HACHETTE

WINE

GUIDES

how to taste wine

how to taste wine

BY PIERRE CASAMAYOR

CASSELL ILLUSTRATED

C O N T E N T S

Discovering...
Tasting

The art of tasting, in contrast to the act of drinking, is a question of measure: it teaches you how to put quality before quantity. And because it stimulates all the senses – sound, sight, smell, taste and touch – it is an invitation to hedonism.

Tasting is not simply drinking

The pleasure of the senses is essentially an animal pleasure. It is the physical excitement associated with a natural desire such as eating or drinking, for example. If taste were not a source of pleasure, who knows whether men would stop eating altogether? Wine was originally a drink like any other. Then it was linked with the celebration of mass, and today it ranks as a gastronomic product with an ever-increasing range choose from. Wine is deemed essential to man's survival and, rightly or wrongly, linked with a range of health benefits. This much at least we can say: wine in moderation gives a sense of wellbeing that shows up the world in a kinder light. Excessive drinking, on the other hand, has the opposite effect, ruining the health and dulling the senses. An alcoholic is motivated by need, not a desire for pleasure.

Tasting is analysing

The pleasure of tasting wine could remain strictly sensory were it not for our memory and cultural education. One of the attractions of tasting is the fun of analysis: identifying an aroma or singling out one aroma from a host of others; making the connection with other sensory and cultural pleasures;

Assessing a wine's colour, aromas and flavours is part of the pleasure of wine tasting.

recognising a certain style of wine or identifying a particular vintage; experiencing the supreme delight that takes you far beyond the world of the senses into the realm of the spirit. As a taster of wines from all

Blending Krug Champagne

How to recognise quality

What are quality factors? What is the difference between a good wine and a great wine? The question is not quite so superfluous as it might seem at first, despite the undeniable quality and status of the leading wine estates. Wine, after all, is not an industrial product solely defined by the winemaking technique. It also depends on weather conditions throughout the growth cycle of the vine, right up to the point of harvest. Of all agricultural products, wine is unique; none is so widely talked about, so inspiring, so individual in every case. Wine has given rise to so many fine distinctions that it no longer counts as a food but as a subject of cultural interest in its own right. Some of the greatest wines have evolved slowly over the centuries, the result of years of Old World traditions. Others have emerged more quickly using the modern techniques now available to New World vineyards. But is there a tried and tested recipe that can produce a great wine anywhere in the world?

Advances in oenology have made it possible to produce good wines on any soil that is suitable for vine cultivation. Universally popular grape varieties almost unfailingly yield good commercially produced wines, with a bouquet based on the varietal characteristics of the grape, plus toasty or peppery touches added by a touch of oak ageing. In every case, they are made according to the same basic formula: a combination of state-of-the-art technology and an aggressive marketing policy.

The approach becomes infinitely more complex when the aim is to express the origins of the wine and the *terroir* (the growing environment) in which it was produced. With experience we learn how to find the right words to describe the elegance or the particular taste of a great wine, and with this experience it becomes clear that a wine is only truly great if it expresses its *terroir*. In the world of viticulture, it is as if the soil itself had rights.

over the world, you can draw comparisons with a wealth of past experiences hidden deep in your memory like a virtual library. Tasting becomes a magical journey in time and space, for the price of a few drops of wine.

Tasting is communicating

Novices might sometimes wonder whether tasting is a sufficient pleasure in itself; or whether, indeed, our efforts to describe the myriad of sensations do not take the edge off the pleasure of drinking wine. Why bother with expert comments when all we need to say is whether or not we think a wine is any good, and whether we like the taste of it or not? The fact is that wine tasting is similar to analysing a poem or criticising a painting.

First impressions are fine for a while but they tend to lack a deeper insight. A museum guide can reveal aspects of a painting that you could not even have guessed at. Similarly, literary criticism sheds light on the mysteries of the written word. Pleasure is always said to be heightened by knowledge. To describe the wine in depth is to prolong the cultural enjoyment of it, a product of humble agricultural origin. A glass of wine tells a unique story, represents a particular technique, recalls times past and conjures up a variety of different images. It reveals a process of trial and error inspired by one man's genius. Expressing all these things is the culmination of tasting pleasure – it's almost a literary pleasure that transforms each glass of wine into a celebration of the senses.

What is a great wine?

A wine's true character originates with the vine. Premium-quality grapes are therefore essential for a great wine. Moreover, because a quality wine must express its native *terroir*, the way it is cultivated must be environmentally friendly (the ploughing methods used, ecologically sound pesticides and fungicides, controlled yields, and so on).

The secret of a great *cuvée* lies in selecting the pick of the crop from one estate and mixing together the various wines from these grapes to produce a superior final blend. To achieve this, wine producers must be prepared to discard a fair amount of their wine at no mean expense.

TASTING BRIEF

How to distinguish between two wines

• **Tasting a pair of wines**
Compare two samples in no particular order. Begin by asking yourself whether the samples are identical, or whether there are noticeable differences. Now try and describe the differences.

• **Tasting a trio of wines**
Compare three glasses of wine, two of which contain exactly the same wine. Taste all three wines in no particular order and see if you can identify the odd one out.

Producing premium-quality wines depends on complicated factors at every level. The raw material must either be a careful blend of grapes grown in different vineyard plots, or if the wine is to be made from a single grape variety (*monocépage*), must rely on the quality of individual plants of the same variety from the same estate. Naturally occurring yeasts also give rise to an abundance of distinctive flavours and aromas. The maturing process contributes significantly, especially the harmonious influence of oak from various sources. Thereafter, the wine depends for its balance on the finesse of the fruit and the silky texture of the tannins. A great *cuvée* always achieves that miraculous combination of

concentrated body and elegance, culminating in a gustatory and tactile sensation that may be described as *fondu* (smoothness). Lastly, it is length on the palate that ultimately separates a good wine from a great wine; a great wine always has length. The quality of a *cuvée* is also reflected in its ability to age: every fine wine, white or

Professional tastings

A professional tasting is always designed to achieve a specific purpose using certain methods of assessment, particularly grading and statistics. Amateur tastings can sometimes follow the same approach.

There are two types of professional tasting:
• Technical tastings judge how different methods of vinification and maturing have influenced the taste of the wine. Sensory analysis may be used to identify selected elements only, or to study the wine as a whole. Technical tastings are carried out all year round by oenologists, cellar masters and *vignerons*. One of the most commonly carried out is the *dégustation d'assemblage*, or blending tasting, when the different blends of *cuvées* are sampled.
• Classification or competition tastings classify wines according to quality, for the purposes of marketing and publicity. Tastings such as these are organised by various official bodies, wine guides and specialist magazines. They are also fun to try at home.

The quality of the wine depends on the care taken with the grape (detail of a carving from a barrel of Mercier Champagne, 1889).

red, will have an impressive collection of legendary vintages to its credit.

There is a delicate balance to be maintained. When human error upsets this, even great wines from exceptional *terroirs* go into decline until a talented *vigneron* restores them to their former glory.

Are competition wines also good drinking wines?

There are now countless 'blind' tastings (when the bottle is covered so that taster has no idea what it is) of wines of every *appellation* and nationality. Some are genuine quality wines, others are impostors with flashy names. The winners of this type of promotional or media event tend to be the wines with the greatest concentration, the fruitiest bouquet, the highest alcohol content and the most pronounced tannins. In short, excess impresses, not balance. It would be wrong to question the integrity of the verdict, however revolutionary it might be, but it comes as no surprise to find that great *cuvées* are often beaten on such occasions. Legendary wines like Mouton, Petrus and Yquem are repeatedly passed over in favour of wines that no one has heard of. Serve these wines at table to the same jury, however, and the result would probably look quite different. One sip of the prize-winning wines is often enough, while the classic wines slip down effortlessly. That, after all, is what a keen wine drinker really seeks.

The reputation of Napa Valley in California is based on Cabernet Sauvignon.

TASTING BRIEF

How to rank a series of wines
When the objective is to establish a hierarchy of wines, it is best to compare similar wines from the same appellation or, failing that, wines from the same region. This allows tasters to form a precise idea of the ideal wine profile.

Discovering...
What wine is made up of?

Thanks to modern methods of chemical and biochemical analysis, we are constantly discovering new compounds in wine. Although we are still a long way from knowing all the secrets of wine, we have at least succeeded in isolating eight fundamental elements which have an influence on the taste of wine. Tasting is the sensory identification of these compounds based on colour, aroma and balance.

Water

Wine is composed of 80-90 per cent water of vegetable origin, the quantity varying according to the alcohol content.

Alcohol

Ethyl alcohol is produced by the action of yeasts on sugar, and accounts for 8–20 per cent of a wine's volume. There is also a tiny amount of methyl alcohol showing the presence of pectin in the grapes (from the pips). Glycerol, a tri-hydric alcohol formed by the fermenting sugars, is present in varying quantities. Alcohol gives the wine its warmth. Together with the sugars, it also helps to make a wine *moelleux* (sweet), rich and viscous

Acids

Acids may be contained in the grapes (tartaric, malic, citric and gluconic acid) or produced by fermentation (lactic, succinic and acetic acid). Total acidity varies from 2–7 grams/litre (expressed as sulphuric acid). Some acids have a specific aroma. Acids are the main source of the acid flavour that is one of the fundamental tastes of wine (see p.46), increasing the production and fluidity of saliva.

Dégorgement (disgorgement) is uncorking the bottle to eject the dépôt (sediment) of dead yeasts from the second fermentation.

Polyphenols and phenolic compounds

Phenols can be divided into two main groups:
• Pigments: flavonols, or yellow pigments, and anthocyanins (200-500 grams/litre) or red pigments (see p.26).
• Tannins (1–3 grams/litre) contained in the grape skins and pips or derived from the wood of the casks. Tannins have a characteristic astringency that puckers the mucous membranes of the mouth. They thicken the saliva and can make the wine seem dry on the palate. Excessive tannins lead to bitterness (see p.48). In the course of ageing, tannins combine with the anthocyanins (stabilising the colour) and undergo condensation (decreasing the astringency).

Sugars

Finished wine contains a certain proportion of non-fermented sugars called *residual* sugars (glucose, fructose, arabinose and xylose). Dry wines should contain no more than two grams/litre of residual sugars whereas sweet wines may contain as much as 300 grams/litre. They contribute basic sweetness, add to the viscosity (**see p.46**) and help form the 'tears' (**see p.29**). Sugar and alcohol together create richness and a mellow creaminess known as *moelleux*. This describes a wine without excessive sweetness but unctuous and slightly viscous on the palate.

Salty substances

Sugar and alcohol disguise the flavour of various ions that would otherwise taste salty. Potassium, sodium, chlorides, sulphates and tartrates are all detectable in wine.

Carbon dioxide

Wine contains variable amounts of carbon dioxide. It is detectable at concentrations of 500–600 mg/litre and leads to bubbles at levels of over1,000 mg/litre. Carbon dioxide adds freshness by accentuating acidity. It also diffuses the aromas

Aromatic substances

These account for the richness and complexity of a wine. They belong to very different chemical families classified as aromatic because of their volatility. Alcohol, aldehydes, esters, fatty acids and terpenes, however minute their quantities, contribute odours that recall the natural world. The terms used to describe these odours are known as *analogous*. Acetate isoamylate, for instance, which is present in wines produced by carbonic maceration, is said to contribute notes of acid drops. Phenylethylic alcohol adds notes of roses, glycyrrhizine adds suggestions of liquorice, cinnamic aldehyde adds hints of cinnamon – the list goes on. These are the substances that give a wine its aroma. Some are olfactory, some are retro-olfactory (**see p.31**). The combination or juxtaposition of several of these will influence the range of aromas in a wine, emphasising some and eliminating others.

Organising...
The setting for the wine tasting

Organising a wine tasting is like preparing for any celebration. This is, after all, a celebration of the senses, pleasure and conviviality. As with all such occasions, though, this ceremony requires planning, and a few common-sense rules apply.

Getting the conditions right

Professional wine tastings are held in rooms where the heat, humidity and especially the light are controlled. Tasters are isolated from each other in individual booths, each one containing its own light source and spittoon. Amateur wine tasters, however, often have to make do with less-than-ideal conditions, either at home or in a wine-tasting club.

It is essential to choose the right time to carry out the tasting. Our senses are keenest just before meals and dullest during meals or, worse still, when we are digesting food. Wines should therefore be tasted between 10am and 12pm or between 6 and 8pm. The only food allowed during tastings are small pieces of bread. These can be nibbled to remove the tannic or acid taste that often builds up in the mouth when several wines are tasted in succession. Appetisers, olives and cheese are forbidden as they often disguise defects in wine. The tasters should also be in good health as colds, flu, stomach upsets or simple fatigue can have an effect on judgement. Each taster has to sample a reasonable number of wines to maintain a sharp sense of discrimination.

Tasting at home

• Choose a well-lit room for your tasting, preferably with good natural light. If the tasting is to be held at night, use 'daylight' lighting.

• Cover the table with a white tablecloth or, failing that, place a sheet of white paper in front of each of your guests.

• The room temperature should be as it was in the 19th century when the term *chambrer*, meaning to bring wines up to room temperature, was coined. It

referred to a room temperature of 18–20°C (64.4–68°F).

• Avoid any odours that are likely to interfere with the tasting – smoke, flowers, fruit bowls – and close the kitchen door.The tasters should not wear perfume or lipstick.

• There is no need for absolute silence during a tasting, but make sure nothing disturbs the guests' concentration.

Preparing the bottles and glasses

• The day before, transfer the wine to the tasting room. An hour before the tasting is due to begin, stand the youngest wines upright and uncork them. When you bring the oldest bottles up from the cellar, replace them in their original positions without turning them or standing them upright. Uncork them in a basket, being careful not to shake them. Decant them if there is too much sediment.

• Prepare a sufficient number of spittoons: plastic containers do just as well as champagne buckets.

• Choose the right shape of glass. A stem glass is essential to keep the hand as far as possible from the nose and to prevent the smell of

Each glass is shaped to bring out the qualities of particular wines. Glasses in the *Les Impitoyables* range (right) will show up the slightest defect.

● T A S T I N G B R I E F
The role of the glass

Choose a fairly aromatic wine such as a white Sauvignon Blanc. Pour into glasses and containers of different shapes: a tasting cup, a beer glass, a glass mustard pot, a Champagne glass (*coupe*), a round wine glass, a tulip glass and a glass in the *Les Impitoyables* series. The impression on the nose will vary. Repeat the experiment before and after the wine is swirled.

the skin from interfering with the appreciation of the wine. The glass should be held by the base. A good wine-tasting glass should satisfy the following requirements:

– it should be fine and transparent to reveal all nuances of colour;

– it should be tulip-shaped or ovoid (egg-shaped) with an opening narrow enough to concentrate the bouquet, but wide enough to release the aromas;

– it should be tall enough to allow the wine to be easily swirled.

The tasting glass approved by the French standards organisation (AFNOR) is the INAO glass. Other tasting glasses have specific shapes designed to suit a particular type of wine: white wine, young or old red wine, sparkling wine or eau-de-vie. Examples include professional tasting glasses, *Les Impitoyables* and the Riedel range. Certain types of glass, generally reserved for

technical tastings, concentrate the bouquet to such a degree that they act like stills accentuating the defects as much as the qualities of the aromas. Each taster should be provided with several glasses. The glass should be filled to no more than a third, leaving room for the aromas to circulate. So-called 'tasting cups' are unsuitable as they do not allow a proper appreciation of the colour or the aromas.

• Wash the glasses in lightly soapy water. Rinse thoroughly with clean water and hang them upside down to dry in a well-aired room. Before commencing any tasting, smell the glass and 'season' it (rinse it) with the first of the wines to be tasted.

Uncorking the bottle

There is a knack to this delicate operation but the right corkscrew is essential. While there is a plethora of outlandish devices on the market today, the most widely used corkscrews have a screw-lever action. These come in various shapes and sizes, ranging from 'folksy', awkward corkscrews with a handle shaped like a vine plant, to the professional 'waiter's friend' with a lever that bears down on the bottleneck. Some models have a dual-action lever which is useful for drawing long corks. Some have a silicon-coated worm that slides effortlessly into the cork without damaging it. Avoid using corkscrews with two side arms as it can be difficult to keep the worm straight. The revolutionary Screw-Pull corkscrew has its origins in traditional wooden or metal corkscrews that are based on the Archimedean endless screw. Screw-Pull corkscrews are easy to use, even by beginners, but they look rather inelegant and have the

There are many types of corkscrew From left to right: a pronged cork retriever, the Screw-Pull corkscrew and the 'waiter's friend'.

disadvantage of splitting the cork. Cork retrievers with two prongs that slide either side of the cork are efficient but require a certain amount of dexterity. They are invaluable for drawing very old corks that might crumble if pulled by conventional corkscrews. Avoid gimmicky devices such as gas-operated corkscrews (which in any case seem to have vanished, like most other useless gadgets). Whatever your choice of corkscrew, the following rules apply:

• Remove the foil capsule using either the blade on the corkscrew or the little cutting wheels (whichever is applicable). Slice the capsule either above or beneath the ring of the bottleneck. A good *sommelier* (wine waiter) should be able to slice it through the centre of the ring although this is done mainly for effect. Wax-sealed bottles may look impressive but they can be a disaster to uncork, splattering little pieces of wax all over the tablecloth. It is better by far to remove the wax beforehand by striking it with the handle of a knife.

• Clean the top of the cork with a tea towel to remove any traces of mould.

• Insert the worm straight into the centre of the cork. Drive it well in, but on no account let it go right through the cork.

• Gradually loosen the cork, easing it out gently and smoothly.

• Clean the bottleneck once again and smell the cork to check for any abnormal odours. For presentation purposes, the cork may be attached to the decanter or the serving basket.

Stubborn Champagne corks can be removed with purpose-designed pincers. If the cork splits in two, leaving the body of the cork in the bottleneck, then remove it with a corkscrew.

Opening a bottle of Champagne

This is challenging as it depends entirely on dexterity. Providing all goes well (see caption above) you do not normally need a corkscrew. Start by slicing through the foil capsule beneath the muzzle. Untwist the eyelet of the muzzle, but do not remove it. Holding the cork and muzzle in one hand and the base of the bottle in the other, turn the bottle not the cork. Hold the cork down so carbon dioxide is released slowly. Any mousse that does gush out onto the bottleneck should be poured off into a separate glass. Hold the bottle by the base as you serve the Champagne.

Organising...
Serving wines at table

Learning how to approach wine at mealtimes is an essential part of improving your wine-tasting expertise. This includes choosing the right wines and serving them correctly.

Wine is mainly drunk as an accompaniment to a meal. Right: *Le Déjeuner d'Huitres* **by Jean-François De Troy (1735).**

Tasting wine at table

Generally speaking, the gustatory sensations of food last longer than those of wine. If the food flavours are overpowering, they can destroy the first impression of the wine. Even bland dishes will influence the taste of the wine by highlighting certain constituents. Strongly flavoured dishes, on the other hand, will dampen the alcoholic effects of the wine, while fatty dishes will obliterate its tannins. Spicy food can strip wine of all its character, reducing it to a drink like any other. As a taster, you can choose between tasting a wine on its own or combining it with food. You may wish to discover the intrinsic qualities of a wine for your own enjoyment, or you may have professional reasons for doing so (such as a commentary to write). To keep your impressions of the wine separate from those of the food, taste it before eating, and always rinse your mouth with water beforehand, or chew a piece of bread. This is important to remove the taste of the previous dish. Alternatively, for a more hedonistic tasting aimed at savouring the combined effect of a particular

wine and dish, take a mouthful of the food, followed by a sip of the wine. As you do so, observe the interaction between the two and whether they inspire harmonious or contrasting sensations. When the dish is finished, it is always interesting to taste the wine once again and allow the sensations to dissipate slowly in the mouth. The impression of the wine is now dominant, with the food in a supporting role.

Serving wines in the right order

Sommelier schools agree that there are two basic strategies when combining gourmet foods with wine. One is to combine a particular dish with a particular wine, regardless of the other dishes. The aim here is to create a harmony of strength, finesse and aromas – combining a tannic red wine with red meat, for example. Or, you can create a meal based on a succession of courses and complementary wines. Because the senses become duller as the meal progresses, the wines should be served in order of strength: white wines before red wines, light wines before tannic wines, simple wines before complex wines, young wines before old wines, dry wines before sweet wines. This assumes, of course, that the courses follow a similar progression of strength and richness; if not, there can be problems. For instance, the traditional pairing of foie gras and sweet wine served at the start of a

A wine to match every cheese (opposite) – red wines with hard cheese, lively white wines with goat's cheese and sweet wines with blue cheese.

meal is a powerful combination that can significantly prejudice your impressions of the red wine that follows. Instead, do as the Romans did under Lucullus: save the foie gras for the end of the meal and serve the Sauternes with the Roquefort. You can also cut down on the required number of courses by serving a glass of water or a *sorbet* (rather than an *eau-de-vie*) to remove the taste of the previous dish and wine.

To avoid such difficulties, meals are increasingly planned around a single wine. This is certainly much simpler when eating out in a restaurant but extremely challenging when it comes to

The art of good wine service: choosing a wine that complements the dish, then serving it correctly.

choosing the right combinations. In this case, the wine dictates the food, not vice versa: the entire meal, from the first course to the dessert, is planned to enhance the qualities of the selected wine.

Serving etiquette

The ceremony of opening and serving wine is governed by certain rules of etiquette and requires some dexterity. It forms part of the training given to professional wine waiters (*sommeliers*) at hotel school, and is a feature of every wine-waiting contest. In a restaurant, it is the job of the wine waiter to present the label to the client, open the bottle at table and invite him or her to taste the wine. The guest now has the dubious honour of deciding, in just a few seconds, whether or not the wine is any good, or whether there is something wrong with it – such as the dreaded taste of cork, for example. This decision has serious

consequences, particularly if an expensive bottle of wine then has to be discarded, much to the dismay of the wine waiter. Such misfortunes, however, can befall even the most illustrious *cuvée*. Ultimately, it is a restaurant's duty to keep the customer satisfied. The guest, who is assumed to be a person of good breeding, should always have the last word.

The classic method of serving wine is the 'pincer' method, holding the base of the glass with two fingers (the pincers). The waiter lifts it slightly, together with the bottle or decanter, tilting the glass towards the bottle as the wine is poured. The glass is then replaced in front of the guest's plate. The bottle is held in the left hand and the glass in the right. A white napkin on the waiter's right sleeve is designed to catch any drops that might stain the white tablecloth. The glass should be half filled, to just above the point where the glass narrows.

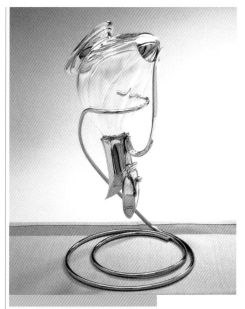

Washing glasses and decanters

Few things are more unpleasant than a glass smelling of detergent or damp tea towel – assuming, of course, that they don't smell of the cupboard or the box in which they are kept. Glasses and decanters should be washed in boiling water, rinsed in plenty of cold water and left to drip dry, upside-down, on a draining rack. Rinse them once again before the meal. Never store glasses upside-down on a shelf as this makes them smell stale. Decanters, too, should be stored open, without their stoppers. Tarnished decanters can be de-scaled with spirits of salt, vinegar or coarse salt and rinsed in plenty of running water. Always rinse them with wine before decanting.

Right: glasses from the collection of Château Pichon-Longueville collection belonging to the Comtesse de Lalande (Pauillac).

The fashion today among young *sommeliers*, although not the older generation, is to hold the bottle by the base. It is then frequently placed to one side on a sideboard or in an ice bucket, often out of reach of the guest, who can sometimes almost die of thirst waiting for the *sommelier* to replenish the glasses!

You can dispense with the ceremony at home, but good etiquette is still important. Be sure to taste the wine in private before serving it at table. Although it is customary for the host to serve the wine, you are not expected to leave your place to do so. Allow a friend sitting at the other end of the table to do the honours. Female guests are served first, of course, starting with those on the right of the host and followed by those on the left. Male guests are served in clockwise order, starting with the male guest in position of honour on the right of the hostess. This is what all the best books say, but what you do in practice is largely a matter of common sense depending on the occasion. To prevent unsightly wine stains on the tablecloth, use special drip collars fitted onto the bottleneck. They are available from wine merchants and goldsmiths.

Showing the wine to best effect

The objects surrounding wine and the serving of wine are no longer purely practical. Today they fulfil a more decorative role and add to the gastronomic pleasure of the occasion. They play an important part in any meal with wine at its centre, by drawing attention to the star of the show. That said, you do not need to invest in costly museum pieces.

• To prevent drips while pouring the wine, use a **drip catcher**. There are two types, both equally efficient: a slim metal insert that slips into the bottleneck, or a collar that fits around it.

• **Bottle mats** are also essential to keep the tablecloth clean. Most are made of silver but some are of pewter or cork.

• **Pourer baskets** allow venerable, ancient wines to be left on their sides as they were in the cellar. If you do decide to keep to this principle, remember that it is difficult to uncork a bottle on its side. Serving the wine, on the other hand, is easier from a pourer basket, thanks to the handle. Pourer baskets are made of wicker or silver.

• **Ice buckets**, crucial for keeping both white and red wine at the right temperature, are often little works of art, often in silver-plate or

Storing an opened bottle of Champagne

Champagne is more delicate than still wine because the carbon dioxide has a nasty habit of escaping from the bottle. Forget about such gadgets as little spoons and other similar nonsense: you need a purpose-designed stopper that clamps onto the neck of the bottle. Even that, however, cannot retain the bubbles indefinitely, make sure you finish the bottle at the first opportunity.

crystal. They are usually placed on a small sideboard next to the table. When choosing an ice bucket, remember the job it has to do and pick one that is tall enough to immerse the bottleneck. Large capacity buckets designed to hold several bottles are useful during wine-tasting meals.

• **Wine thermometers** are rather ostentatious but a must for any serious wine lover. There are many to choose from, either with a cork or a metal head. Some are beautifully boxed. Digital thermometers that stick onto the bottle are as inefficient as they are ugly and should be avoided.

• **Bottle holders for six bottles** can also look handsome next to the table. These can be made of wood, wicker or metal, but should never be made of plastic.

Storing uncorked bottles

Moderate drinkers may often find that a bottle is still half full at the end of a meal. It would be a crime to discard what remains, particularly when the following day might reveal aspects of the wine that passed unnoticed during the meal. To protect the wine from rapid oxidation, simply replace the cork in the neck the right way up and store the bottle in a cool, dark place. The wines at greatest risk of spoiling are those with the most aromatic bouquet: young white wines and red *primeur* ('newborn', i.e. very young) wines have a tendency to lose their exuberance and complexity quickly. White wines for laying down, and mature red wines, may also lose some or most of their vigour, but a few live to fight another day. On the other hand, certain austere, closed wines – such as young, white Chenin or young, tannic reds – seem to develop even further, revealing a charm and a complexity that remained hidden on the first visit. Every wine is unique and there are always surprises in store. You can help to prolong the life of a bottle by using an ingenious kit that consists of a special rubber stopper and a small vacuum pump (Vac-u-Vin). After placing the stopper in the bottle, the air is pulled out using the pump. The equipment is widely available from specialised shops.

Organising...
Serving wines at the right temperature

It is essential to serve wine at the right temperature to enhance its qualities. However, to bring out the best in a wine, it should reach its ideal temperature gradually, with no sudden shocks. Tempting though it may be to rush the process, never chill a wine in the freezer, and never warm it up in the microwave!

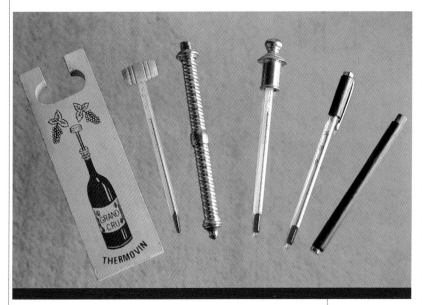

A wine thermometer is essential for monitoring the temperature of the wine in the glass.

Remember – wine warms up in the glass

White wines are generally served too cold, which kills off the aromas and makes them harsh and closed. Red wines, on the other hand, are often served too warm; it is easy to forget that 'room temperature' in cities these days is often too high for this often-cited guide to apply. As a result, the tannins appear dry and the alcohol badly incorporated. The problem is not so much the temperature of the bottle as the temperature of the glass. Such a small volume of liquid soon warms up once it comes in contact with the ambient temperature. So it is better to serve the wine on the cool side (the room is often warmer than the wine) and monitor its progress by placing a wine thermometer in the glass, even though this may raise a smile among guests. A great red wine may be divine at 18°C (64.4°F) and unbalanced at 22°C (71.6°F); an over-heated dining-room can destroy it in a matter of minutes. The only foolproof way of avoiding such catastrophes is to use an ice bucket for white and red wines alike. Make sure you always have one to hand, filled with water and a few ice-cubes, immersing and removing the bottles as often as you need to. This is much more difficult when using a carafe, so wines should be cooler when decanted to allow for the subsequent rise in temperature. You can also decant them beforehand and store them in a cool place. Wine coolers, many of them earthenware, do not control the temperature of the wine, but do stop the bottle from heating up so quickly.

TASTING BRIEF

A regional guide

• Spanish red wines should be served at 16–18°C (60.8–64.4°F) to balance their fullness; white wines should be brought to 8–10°C (46.4–50°F) to emphasise their freshness.

• The same applies to Italian wines. Be careful not to serve the red wines overly cool, or they will appear too lively.

• Chilean and Argentinean red wines, however, can be served cooler at 15–16°C (50–60.8°F).

• Dry white German and Austrian wines should be brought to temperatures of 12–14°C (53.6–57.2°F) and the sweet wines to 10–12°C (50–53.6°F). Swiss wines prefer temperatures of 8-10°C (46.4–50°F).

• Californian and Australian wines should be served at the same temperatures as French wines, perhaps slightly cooler.

Temperature chart

	Examples	Temperature
WHITE WINES		
Dry wines for laying down	Corton, Montrachet, Meursault; Pessac-Léognan, Graves;Californian Chardonnay; Australian Chardonnay; New Zealand Sauvignon Blanc	12°C (50–53.6°F)
Light dry wines	Alsace-Sylvaner, Bordeaux Blanc, Entre-Deux-Mers, Petit-Chablis; Muscadet; Vinho Verde; Italian Soave and Trebbiano d'Abruzzo; German Silvaner; Austrian Grüner Veltliner; Californian Sauvignon Blanc	10 °C (46.4–50°F)
Sparkling wines	Champagne, crémant wines, Blanquette-de-Limoux; Spanish cava; German sekt; Italian asti	8–10°C (46.4–50°F)
Deluxe sparkling *cuvées*	Champagne ; cava	10–12°C (50–53.6°F)
Sweet wines	Sauternes, Barsac, Loupiac, Ste-Croix-du-Mont, Monbazillac, Coteaux-du-Layon, Quarts-de-Chaume; Tokay; German & Austrian Eiswein, Beerenauslesen, Trockenbeerenauslesen, Romanian Cotnari, South African Vin de Constance	8–10°C (46.4–50°F)
Vins doux naturels and *vins de liqueur*	Muscat-de-Rivesaltes, Muscat-de-Lunel, Muscat-de-St-Jean-de-Minervois, Rivesaltes; Muscat-du-Cap-Corse; Greek Lemnos and Samos Muscats; Spanish Moscatel	8°C
RED WINES		
Tannic wines	Pauillac, Margaux, St-Emilion, Pomerol, St-Estèphe, Pommard, Morey-St-Denis, Nuits-St-Georges, Volnay, Mercurey; Châteauneuf-du-Pape; Hermitage; Cahors, Madiran; Bandol; Coteaux-du-Languedoc, Corbières, Fitou, Minervois; Californian Cabernet Sauvignon; Australian Shiraz; Italian Barolo, Chianti Classico, Brunello di Montalcino, Vino Nobile de Montepulciano, Taurasi; Spanish Priorato, Rioja, Ribera del Duero	16-18°C (60.8–64.6°F)
Light wines	Beaujolais; Alsace-Pinot Noir; Anjou; Chinon; Bourgueil and St-Nicolas-de-Bourgueil; Saumur-Champigny; Swiss Dôle; German Spätburgunder; Italian Bardolino and Valpolicella; Spanish Jumilla and Rioja Joven	14-16°C (57.2-60.8°F)
*Primeurs**	Beaujolais Nouveau; Touraine wines	10-12°C (50-53.6°F)
Vins doux naturels and *vins de liqueur*	Banyuls, Maury; Port, Madeira	14-15°C (57.2-59°F)
ROSÉ WINES		
Light wines	Loire rosé	8-10°C (46.4-50°F)
More robust wines	Côtes-de-Provence, Tavel	11-12°C (51.8-53.6°F

*('newborn' or young wines)

Organising...
Decanting

Decanting serves two purposes. The first objective is to separate the wine from any sediment. The second is to 'air' the wine by allowing oxygen to come into contact with it – decanting, and the transfer from bottle to decanter does this efficiently. Opening the bottle in advance serves little purpose as the surface area of the bottleneck is too small for the wine to air properly. It will only diminish certain unpleasant odours (such as a corked or sulphurous smell).

Art and technique

Decanting a wine is essential when the sediment is clearly visible through the bottle. But the right technique is important. The bottle should be carried up from the cellar carefully in a basket or by hand. Before moving it, make a mark with chalk on the upper-side of the bottle to ensure that you do not inadvertently turn it round and disturb the sediment – which would be disastrous. With a light source in front of you, usually a candle or a naked bulb, gently tilt the bottle and pour the wine carefully into the decanter. You can also use special decanting cradles that tilt the bottle as you turn the handle, thus ensuring a steady pouring motion. However, these are generally too large to stand on a table and are usually kept in the wine cellar. Stop decanting the wine when the first particle of the sediment reaches the bottleneck.

Decanting old wines

Decanting very old, fragile wines is a much more delicate operation. After so many years of solitary confinement, sudden exposure to the air can prove fatal for such senior citizens. Nevertheless, these wines do contain significant sediment that must be separated before tasting. The only way to resolve this dilemma is to use a pourer basket that allows the wine to be decanted without coming into contact with air.

Opinions are divided as to whether or not decanting really does air a wine. For some there is no difference between wine served from the bottle and a wine that has just been decanted. The critical factor, however, is the time of decanting. In a restaurant, wines

cannot be decanted until the last moment, and bottles cannot be opened before they are bought (although a good customer may request that a wine be opened in advance). At home there is nothing to prevent you from airing a wine for as long as you like. Only experience will tell you how long that should be.

Decanting young red wines

Airing always has a beneficial effect on young red wines. It reduces the high carbon dioxide levels often found in them, and it acts on the reduction odours that can mask their fruity bouquet. The results of tasting competitions would doubtless be quite different if the wines were decanted rather than tasted within moments of uncorking. As it is, their fate is decided virtually as they leave the bottle, before they have had time to air. Airing during decanting also improves tannin assimilation. Tannins in young wines, for instance, appear less aggressive and better blended after airing. Sadly it can have the opposite effect on some highly aromatic wines, stripping them of much of their complexity. What is beneficial in one case can prove detrimental in another.

If in doubt, you can carry out an experimental tasting – perhaps with friends – before the meal. Open the bottle to be tasted in advance. Pour a little of the wine into a large glass with a wide surface area where the

Decanters

Decanters are an endless source of inspiration to crystal manufacturers and goldsmiths and come in a wide variety of shapes, sizes, styles and prices. They can be made of glass or crystal, ranging from the classically shaped *carafe boule* to 'duck-shaped' decanters, some with attractive spouts and handles in silver or pewter. In fact, each style of decanter is designed for a different purpose. Wide-based decanters are ideal for airing wines; long-necked ones retain the aromas; small decanters fit easily into the cool-box. The 'duck' decanter is a good compromise, especially as it makes a magnificent table piece, but the metal parts are hard to clean. (Everyday silver-cleaning agents should never be used as they might taint the wine.) A funnel, usually of pewter or silver, is invaluable when using a decanter. When not in use, place it on a saucer to avoid staining the tablecloth.

aromas can circulate, and re-cork the bottle. Now prepare to smell the wine in two stages: immediately after pouring and 15 minutes later when the wine has been left to stand in a cool, well-aired place. First impressions indicate what the wine is like straight from the bottle. If you find it improves with airing, decanting is essential. If it deteriorates, leave it in the bottle. If you are familiar with the wine and keep a cellar book, refer to your notes from the previous tasting. These recollections are invaluable when it comes to making a decision.

Generally speaking, a tannic wine (such as a Bordeaux) is more easy to decant than an aromatic wine (such as a Burgundy). It is no accident that you find decanters in the Gironde and baskets in Dijon. The longer the time between decanting and serving, the greater the change in the wine. Bear that in mind when decanting, and adjust the time accordingly. Two hours in advance is about right for a young wine, one hour will suffice for mature wines and barely a few minutes is necessary for volatile wines.

Decanting white wines

Experience shows that some white wines are improved by decanting, even though it is not the usual practice to do so. Young, lively, zippy wines have everything to lose, but wines for laying down, especially those vinified in casks, will improve in expression, harmony and smoothness. Decanting is essential in the case of white Graves and Pessac-Léognan wines, and it also helps to open up certain Chenin wines – these tend to lose their initial reticence and become beautifully eloquent. Even the great Chardonnays and Burgundies become more complex with decanting. Champagne can be decanted into sparkling cut-crystal, which looks stunning on the table. What the wines lose in bubbles they gain in fruitiness. That said, only decant the less illustrious Champagnes: the great *cuvées* should be served straight from the bottle. Sweet wines should definitely be decanted, preferably a long time in advance, and set aside in a cool dark place. Airing has the added advantage of eliminating sulphur dioxide, which can cause headaches.

25

Assessing...
The 'eye' of the wine

The first step of a wine tasting is to assess the appearance, or 'eye', of the wine. This tells you something about how the wine was made and how well it has kept, and also indicates its age and alcohol content. Sight, therefore, is the taster's first contact with the wine and the first source of attraction. The eye of a wine is judged in terms of colour, brightness and intensity.

First impressions

It is not always easy to distinguish a light red wine from a rosé – or even from a rich and opulent white wine when you are blindfolded. This can be an amusing game to play at home, provided you are prepared to get it wrong most of the time. Nobody can deny that

Judging the quality of the vinification and ageing from the appearance of the wine.

colour is of great importance when you are appraising a wine. A limpid, radiant white, for instance, is immediately praiseworthy. A deep, dark red suggests depth, but too little intensity will probably lead the taster to criticise the nose and palate.

the case of a Côtes-de-Provence, but a developed wine in the case of a Bergerac. A rosé made by *pressurage* (from pressing red grapes) is pale-coloured. A rosé made by partial maceration appears more intense. Young rosé wines, and those based on Syrah or Tannat grapes, reveal traces of blue; older wines, or those rich in Grenache, have elements of brown.

Red wines

The range of predominantly red shades in wines is due to the development of the anthocyanins. Young wines contain free anthocyanins that present as intense elements of blue. These eventually combine with red to create shades of purplish-blue. With age, the anthocyanins blend with the tannins to create elements of yellow – these are seen in the glass as orange highlights. Later the colour becomes deeper overall, verging on brown. Likewise, a wine may be a particular colour around the meniscus (at the surface of the wine): a ruby-coloured wine, for example, can have a meniscus with an orange border.

The depth of colour depends on the grape variety from which the wine is made. Gamay yields light cherry-coloured wines, while a wine of the same age based on Cabernet Sauvignon is a deeper ruby colour. The only signs of its youth are the crimson shades around the meniscus.

White wines

White wines are basically yellow but they develop successive shades of green or brown with age. Young wines tend to have a greenish hue whereas old wines take on shades of brown. Between the two, there is an array of colours including pale yellow, golden-yellow, buttercup, topaz, antique gold (old wines and sweet wines), honey-coloured, russet, tawny, copper and amber.

Rosé wines

The colour of a rosé wine depends on the grape variety, local winemaking traditions and age. An orange-pink shade suggests a rather young wine in

TASTING BRIEF

• **To judge intensity**, pour a deeply coloured wine into several glasses and add 20, 40, 50 and 80 per cent water respectively. Rearrange the glasses in ascending order according to colour intensity. For a better appraisal of the intensity of colour of a red wine, move a pencil tip up and down behind the glass and observe its image across the meniscus. See how much weaker the image appears above and below the meniscus. With practise, using the same glass and the same pencil, you can to judge the intensity of colour of any wine. For greater precision during a comparative tasting, compare each sample with a series of glasses arranged in ascending order according to intensity of colour.

• **To judge shade**, pour a white wine into several glasses and, using a pipette, add 1, 2, 5, 10 and 20 drops of red wine. Arrange the glasses in ascending order from the least to the deepest blue.

• **To judge viscosity**, take two glasses, one containing just water, the other water mixed with alcohol (20 per cent) and glycerine (10 grams/litre). Observe the tears that form on the sides of the glass and the appearance of the liquid as you pour it into another glass.

As wine is poured into a glass, the taster can judge its viscosity. Limpidity is observed with the glass held up to candlelight. Brightness and colour are appraised against a white background.

For a better appreciation of intensity of colour, the taster moves a pencil up and down behind the glass.

Stages of analysis

1. Limpidity. To judge a wine's limpidity, hold the glass up to natural or artificial light against a black background. Look at the wine through the glass. If it looks opaque or turbid, the palate is bound to be disappointing: probably rustic, harsh and lacking in finesse.

2. Brightness. A wine's brightness is the degree to which it reflects the light and twinkles like a precious stone. To observe brightness, look at the wine from the top and study the meniscus under natural light against a white background.

3. Colour. This is assessed in two ways: intensity and shade. The intensity of colour is due to the pigment content of a wine (anthocyanins or flavonoids). It depends on the extent to which the wine is light-permeable. Look at the wine from above, with daylight striking the glass from in front, and observe the intensity of the colour as you tilt the glass to adjust the depth of liquid. Bear in mind that intensity varies according to the type of wine: you cannot expect a Beaujolais to be as intensely coloured as an Hermitage, say. To determine the shade of colour, observe the principal tones of a wine's reflections either as it is poured from the bottle or around the rim of the meniscus.

4. Colour around the meniscus. The fine line around the meniscus where the wine meets the glass tells a lot about the development of the wine. This is where the constituents of colour are at their most visible: blue for young wines, brown for old.

5. Viscosity. It used to be thought that a wine's richness (producing the threadlike 'tears' or 'legs' that remain on the inside of a glass) was due to glycerol content. In fact, it is mainly alcohol content that tends to modify the surface tension of the wine, encouraging the formation of droplets on the glass. Observe the viscosity carefully as the wine leaves the bottle.

Analysing shades of colour

FROM YELLOW TO BROWN

Colour	Shade of colour	What can you deduce
WHITE WINES		
	Almost colourless	Very young, protected from oxidation. Modern methods of vinification in tanks
	Very light yellow with green highlights	Young to very young. Vinified and matured in tanks
	Straw-yellow, yellow-gold	Mature. Possibly aged in wood
	Copper-gold, bronze-gold	Already very old
	Amber to black	Oxidised, too old
ROSÉ WINES		
	Stained white wines, *œil-de-perdrix*, pink highlights	Rosé wines made by the *pressurage* method, and young *vins gris*
	Salmon pink to very light, bright red	Young, fruity rosé ready for drinking
	Pink with shades of yellow onion skin	Already quite old for a wine of its type
RED WINES		
	Purplish-blue	Very young. A good shade for Gamays *primeur* wines and Beaujolais Nouveaux (6–18 months old)
	Pure red (cherry)	Optimum development in wines that are neither *primeur* nor for laying down (2–3 years old)
	Red with an orange border	A mature wine of limited ageing ability. A wine that is beginning to age (3–7 years)
	Reddish-brown to brown	Only the really great wines take on this colour at their apogée

FROM LIGHT TO DARK

Colour	Causes	What you can deduce
Too pale	Poor extraction, wet harvest, unrestricted yields, young vines, insufficiently ripe grapes, rotten grapes, insufficient tank fermentation, fermentation at low temperatures	Light wines with poor ageing ability. Wines of minor vintage
Deeply coloured	Good extraction, limited yields, old vines, successful vinification	Good or great wines. Wines with a future

Assessing...
the nose

The assessment of a wine's bouquet is based on a series of impressions known collectively as the 'nose' of the wine. Though countless techniques have been developed to analyse the aromas, no instrument is as powerful as man's sense of smell. Researchers have identified more than 500 different aromas in wine.

We identify the aromas in wine by recalling the odours of the natural world, including the scents of fruit and flowers.

Memorising the aromas

As children, we are taught to see, hear, touch and taste. But although we are born with a highly developed sense of smell, we do nothing to stimulate, train or improve it. It dwindles in some, persists in other and develops differently in each of us. Degrees of sensitivity and olfactory attention vary from one person to another.

As a lover of wine, you will soon learn how to reawaken your sense of smell through practice and memorisation techniques. You will discover how to express your olfactory impressions by drawing analogies between the odours of the world at large and the bouquet of the wine itself. The table of aromas (see p.39) divides odours into six main families: vegetal, floral, fruit, wood, spice and empyreuma.

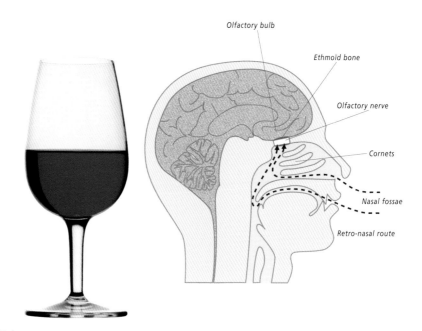

Olfactory bulb

Ethmoid bone

Olfactory nerve

Cornets

Nasal fossae

Retro-nasal route

TASTING BRIEF

The retro-nasal route?

Anyone with a bad head cold loses their sense of taste, which is evidence of the importance of the retro-nasal route in one's sense of smell.

A simple experiment illustrates this. Ask a friend to pinch their nose. Then give them a sip of pineapple juice from a cup (so that they cannot see what they are tasting). They will have great difficulty identifying the fruit in question. As soon as they stop pinching their nose and breathe through it again they will recognise the pineapple flavour.

How the sense of smell works

The eye, the nose and the mouth are all involved in tasting, but of the three the nose definitely plays the starring role. The nose possesses an exceptionally powerful and complex instrument called the olfactory bulb, the centre of olfactory function located in the anterior-inferior region of the brain. The cells devoted to the sense of smell are situated at the top of the nasal fossae and are linked to the bulb by the olfactory nerve which passes through the ethmoid bone (see diagram above). They can be activated by two routes:

• **The direct route**, when you inhale smells through your nose;
• **The retro-nasal route** via the channel that links the palate to the nasal fossae.

The word 'odour' is sometimes used to refer to the impressions received via the direct route and the word 'aroma' to those received via the retro-nasal route, by retro-olfaction. Retro-nasal impressions are perceived orally at the same time as the flavours. The expression of the aromatic components of the bouquet depends on the wine's volatility, which in turn depends on temperature. The nose detects odours in the glass when the wine's temperature ranges from 10-25°C (50-68°F). The aromas are detected retro-nasally in the mouth when the wine's temperature has reached 30°C (86°F) or more. Specialists in olfactory function estimate that brain receptors are capable of distinguishing infinitesimal quantities of 400,000 different odours.

Stages in analysis

The olfactory appraisal of a wine depends on a collection of impressions that experts call the 'nose' of a wine. There are three stages to the process:

1. First, smell the wine as soon as it is poured into the glass (it should be no more than a third full) while holding it perfectly still by the base. You will detect sometimes subtle but fleeting aromas.

2. Swirl the glass and smell the wine once again. You will detect new odours as they are brought forth by airing and oxidation.

3. Agitate the glass to disturb the surface of the wine. This will flush out the less volatile aromas. Then allow the wine to settle in the glass, and check the development of the aromatic components. You will discover that the aromas are far from fixed. The transition from a reductive medium in the bottle to an oxygenated medium in the glass causes the aromatic

components to develop at varying speeds. Smoky and meaty notes, for instance, disappear as soon as the wine is aired.

The last drop

You can learn more about a wine from the last drop remaining at the bottom of the glass. Excessively vegetal or wooded notes become glaringly obvious, as does the wine's volatility. You can also deduce its ageing ability from the quality of its resistance to oxidation. Try warming the glass in one hand while covering it with the other as you would with an old Cognac or Armagnac. Now hazard a guess as to how the wine will develop with age.

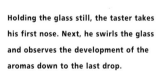

Holding the glass still, the taster takes his first nose. Next, he swirls the glass and observes the development of the aromas down to the last drop.

●

T A S T I N G   B R I E F

Identifying the odours

Pour a selection of fruit juices into opaque glasses. Try to identify each juice from the odour, without seeing the colour. Practise this several times, anou will notice a time delay between receiving two impressions: the nose needs a few seconds to rest before going onto the next glass.

Assessing...
The aromas

Few things are more fascinating than listening to a seasoned taster as they conjure up the aromas in a glass of wine. The ability to put these impressions into words requires a true understanding of the magic of wine, from a ripe, healthy crop of grapes to fermentation and ageing in the bottle.

PRIMARY AROMAS
Grape aromas

Every grape variety has an aromatic signature of variable intensity. Aromatic varieties can be distinguished from those with a more discreet bouquet. The Muscat family represents the height of aroma, but other grape varieties also possess easily recognised aromatic genes. In white wines,for example, aromas of roses and spice are linked with Gewürztraminer, box and white fruits with Sauvignon Blanc. In red wines, notes of pepper and red berries often denote Cabernet Sauvignon, while black-skinned fruits and pepper suggest Syrah. The aromas of a variety can also differ greatly from one region to another – Cabernet Sauvignon from the Médoc has a different aromatic profile from that grown in the Languedoc. Depending on ripeness, Médoc wines develop aromas of peppers, smoke, blackcurrant leaves or ripe blackcurrants. Languedoc wines contribute aromas of fruits in

Left:
Chenin grapes

Below:
ripe Riesling

brandy, and liquorice, on a background of black-skinned fruits. Riesling grapes represent a striking example of the exchange between grape variety and *terroir*. Depending on the soil, they may express delicate floral aromas, or heavier scents of naphtha or truffles. Ripeness is also important. The best proof of this is found in Sauvignon Blanc wines based on early-harvested grapes compared with wines from fully ripe grapes. The former often have unattractive aromas of cat's urine, while the latter have an enticing bouquet of white-fleshed fruits and musk.

Aromas
Primary aromas come from the grape variety. Secondary aromas are derived from fermentation, yeasts and alcohol.

TASTING BRIEF
Identifying the aromas

This is the hardest technique to master. Identifying the aromas challenges the taster's memory or, to put it another way, his or her olfactory knowledge. There are simple exercises which, if practised daily, can help build up this knowledge. Pay attention to the odours around you in the street, the garden, the kitchen, the market, etc. Memorise synthetic aromas and pick them out during the tasting.

• To become thoroughly familiar with the characteristics shared by each aromatic family, try classifying the aromas into categories (floral, fruity, balsamic, empyreumatic, etc.).

• Now smell these aromas 'blind' and identify them. Repeat with each category. Smell the fruity category, for example, and try to name each fruit.

• Identify an aroma chosen at random: say what family it belongs to and what particular aroma it is.

SECONDARY AROMAS
Fermentation aromas

Pure grape juice is not very aromatic. Some of the aromas are present in a latent state as precursors hidden in the skins of the berries. The conversion of sugar into alcohol brings these aromas out with a vengeance: the fruit will only be revealed by fermentation. The agent of conversion is yeast, which produces alcohol and carbon dioxide along with a variety of secondary products, thanks to the enzymes involved in the chemical reaction. These substances complement the initial scents of fruit with secondary aromas which vary according to the type of yeast that is used, the food it feeds off and the temperature of fermentation. The use of 'selected' (exogenous) yeasts can make it possible to determine these aromas. However, it can deprive the wine of a complexity that would otherwise have resulted from fermenting with naturally-occurring yeasts originating in the vineyard or the cellar. Malolactic fermentation softens wines by converting malic acid (which is hard and bitter) into lactic acid. It also produces its own set of aromas which modify the initial scents of fruit: notes of milk and butter combine with the primary aromas.

As they mature in cask, the wines' aromas acquire greater complexity and take on nuances of the wood.
Right: a *bodega* in Jerez.

TERTIARY AROMAS
Maturation aromas

Once all the sugar has been converted into alcohol, the wine is left to mature for varying lengths, depending on the type of wine. Maturation in tanks or barrels is distinct from ageing in the bottle.

• During maturation, the wine remains in a state of controlled oxidation; small quantities of sulphur dioxide are added as an oxidant. Throughout this phase the primary aromas, and the secondary aromas of fermentation, diminish as the wine loses its youthful character. Maturation in tanks helps to seal in all the fruit by protecting the wine from sudden oxidation. Barrel maturation ensures a slow oxidation process. Also, the casks impart fragrant oaky elements to the wine. These vary in strength depending on how toasted, and how old, the oak is.

• Once bottled, the wine enters its reductive state and starts to develop the aromas that come with age: leather, meat and even game, with occasional complex notes of mushrooms, smoke and grilling/roasting. Wine has its own life cycle: birth, development and maturity, followed by decline and death.
Over time, the primary and secondary aromas evolve to form the bouquet, with intermediate stages along the way. A wine that retains some of its original fruitiness after maturation and ageing has every chance of becoming a great wine.

The bouquet, or tertiary aromas

These aromas develop during maturation in tanks or barrels, and in the course of bottle-ageing. Some bouquets have a characteristic taste of oxidation or reduction. Wines of a decent age can also be said to have an aroma of *fumet* (a pleasant smell of meat stock).

Fermentation

This is the process by which yeast cells convert grape sugar into alcohol and carbon dioxide, producing a number of compounds that give the wine its character. To ensure that environmental conditions are right for fermentation, the yeasts need air and a specific temperature, neither too hot nor too cold: 26–30°C (62–86°F) for red wines and 18–20°C (64.4–68°F) for white and rosé wines. Alcoholic fermentation may be followed by secondary or malolactic fermentation. This is triggered by lactic bacteria that convert and deacidify malic acid, lowering levels of natural acidity and transforming the aromas of the wine. To avoid the production of volatile acidity, malolactic fermentation should only take place once all the grape sugar has already been consumed. It may be triggered either in the tank or the cask.

In the glass... the moment of synthesis

When you taste a wine, especially an old wine, the aromas in the glass are not fixed. As the wine starts to exchange the reductive environment of the bottle for the oxidative environment of the glass, its aromatic elements begin to evolve, some faster than others. Any aromas of reduction that are noticeable just after pouring (smokiness and meatiness, for example) disappear as soon as the wine has aired. Likewise, each family of aromas develops at a different pace. Let the wine 'do its own thing'. Your job is to focus on the nose and to concentrate on what the aromas are telling you. Wine with a meal is ideal in this respect as the wine has time to express its many-faceted personality. Experts frequently stress the importance of serving wine at the right temperature as this can modify your perception of the bouquet. Wine served hotter than

Maturation

This comes after fermentation and ensures that the wine is in optimum condition for bottling. Careless maturation can cause numerous defects, such as a dry taste of wood, oxidation, volatile acidity and the proliferation of *brettanomyces* (a strain of yeast).

Reduction

This refers to the evolution of a wine's elements in the airless environment of the sealed bottle. Reduction is characterised by animal aromas and notes of leather, mushrooms and smokiness. Excessive reduction spoils the aromas: red wines acquire a stale musty smell and white wines take on a metallic odour. Reduction may also promote stagnant or putrid smells such as rotten eggs, onions or leeks.

Controlled oxidation

The elements in wine are oxidised on contact with the air. Red wines can be matured in barrels that let the air in slowly. This process produces mellow tannins and also encourages the tannins to combine with the anthocyanins, thus stabilising the colour. White wines, on the other hand, are often protected from the air during maturation. They are usually bottled early, adjusting the dose of sulphur dioxide to preserve the freshness of the aromas. Excessive oxidation causes serious problems: the wines turn an unattractive brown colour and can taste 'cooked', or they take on aromas of Madeira, solvents or varnish.

18°C (64.4°F) rapidly loses its most volatile aromas and is liable to express heavy, unnatural scents.

Honesty and self-confidence

As a taster, you should experience the flavours and aromas for yourself. It is not enough to know what to expect of a wine, or to repeat what your neighbour says. A Meursault should smell of lime blossom, but it may not to you. Your neighbour may have detected a particular aroma, but you may not. The power of suggestion is very persuasive when in the company of a taster of strong character or famous reputation. Stick to your guns. If your fellow tasters insist that there is an aroma of liquorice but you cannot smell it, do not be ashamed to say so. There is nothing like tasting for teaching humility.

TASTING BRIEF

Adding an aromatic element
Each taster takes two glasses of wine and, out of sight of the others, adds an aroma to one of the glasses, preferably in very small quantities. Each person then informs the others of the aroma that has been added. The next step is to identify the aromatic elements in several glasses. The person with the most points is allowed to taste the unadulterated glass of wine.

Aromatic series and aromas

Primary or varietal aromas

WHITE WINES

Floral series	Acacia, hawthorn, carnation, honeysuckle, hyacinth, jasmine, iris, orange blossom, rose, lilac, broom, lime blossom
Vegetal series	New-mown hay, grass, fern, box, cat's urine, herb tea, ivy, tea Aromatic vegetal notes: anise, mint, fennel, etc.
Fruit series	Apple, white or yellow peaches, pear, citrus, lemon, apricot, grapefruit, quince, pineapple, mango, exotic fruits, banana, fresh almonds
Mineral series	Gunflint, chalk, iodine, flint, naphtha or petrol

RED WINES

Floral series	Violet, rose, peony, dried flowers, faded roses
Vegetal series	Green peppers, humus, blackcurrant buds
Fruit series	Red and black fruits (cherries, blackberries, etc.)
Spice series	Pepper, thyme, bay, the *garrigue* (Mediterranean scrubland)

Fermentation aromas

WHITE AND RED WINES

Fermenting series	Yeast, white bread, brioche, biscuit
Milky series	Milk, fresh butter, fondue or hazelnuts, yoghurt
Amylaceous series	Banana, boiled sweets, nail varnish

Maturation aromas

WHITE WINES

Floral series	Dried flowers, camomile, heather
Fruit series	Dried fruit and nuts: hazelnuts, walnuts, almonds, apricots
Sweet series	Honey, praline, marzipan, fruit cake, etc.
Wooded and balsamic series	Oak, new wood, balsam, pine, cedar, vanilla, etc.

RED WINES

Fruit series	Stewed red fruits, plums, black-skinned fruits, black cherries
Empyreumatic series	Cocoa, toast, gingerbread, coffee, tobacco, caramel
Wooded and balsamic series	New wood, oak, pine, eucalyptus, smoky wood, burnt wood, etc.
Spicy series	Vanilla, cinnamon, pepper, cloves, liquorice, strong sweets
Animal series	Meat juices, leather, fur, game, venison, belly of hare
Vegetal series	Undergrowth, mushrooms, truffles
Chemical series	Solvents, varnish, tar

Assessing...
Floral aromas in white wines

The fragrance of vine blossom is the first distinguishable floral aroma to be noted as the wine starts to develop: a discreet, delicate scent of subtlety and finesse. The aromas of dry white wines often have floral undertones, so horticultural language becomes useful as a reference for the taster who is trying to describe them.

Quality of bouquet: a sign of grape ripeness

A wine's quality or richness of aroma corresponds to the ripeness of the grapes used. Green (i.e. under-ripe) grapes express markedly vegetal aromas, leafy notes and the scent of freshly cut grass. Slightly riper grapes show the first signs of floral aromas, yielding wines of greater finesse with a more complex aromatic range. With a few additional months of ageing, the fruity aromas (white fruit in this case) start to kick in, and complete the picture. The most complex bouquets are derived from grapes of peak aromatic maturity as can be readily appreciated in wines based on Sauvignon Blanc. Unripe Sauvignon grapes tend to show a range of vegetal aromas: box, blackcurrant, elder and sage leaves, while perfectly ripe Sauvignon can give a superbly complex bouquet of flowers such as honeysuckle and acacia mingled with fruit (red-fleshed peaches, pears and ripe apples). A white wine can speak the language of flowers, either obviously or subtly, depending on its character.

Meadow flowers

Daisies, buttercups, convolvulus, crocus – the range of meadow flowers is virtually endless. Their aromas bring a particularly refreshing crispness and lightness to a wine. Good examples are wines based on Macabeu, Rolle, Clairette, Grenache Blanc, Viognier, Aligoté and Sylvaner. The heavy, powerful scents of moorland flowers such as broom and heather can be traced in *vins de cépage* (single varietal wines) made from Chardonnay or Marsanne. Finally, the wild flowers of the *garrigue* (the Mediterranean scrubland) add a distinctive scebt to the white wines of southern France.

White flowers

These are the most delicate flowers of all with intense, yet elegant fragrances: acacia, honeysuckle and hawthorn, peach, blossoming fruit trees – apple and cherry – and carnations. This broad range of aromas is characteristic of fine, thoroughbred white wines. Scents of white flowers are distinguishable in wines that are based on grape varieties including Chardonnay, Roussanne, Sauvignon Blanc, Sémillon, Viognier and Riesling.

Citrus flowers

Muscat grapes apart, the aromas of such flowers as orange blossom and citronella are never dominant but they do enhance other fragrances. A touch of citronella brings out the liveliness and lightness of a white wine's bouquet, while a note of orange blossom gives it volume and length.

Roses, lilies and elderflower

Some flowers have a tendency to give off heady, dominating aromas. The best example of this is the marked fragrance of roses in Muscat and Gewürztraminer wines, which can create an impression of fullness, or occasionally heaviness. Exceptionally aromatic grape varieties, especially Riesling, Pinot Gris, Gewürztraminer and Muscat, also present aromas of lilies and elderflower.

Geranium: sign of a flawed bouquet

Excessive sorbic acid, added to white wines to protect them from mould, gives the bouquet an unpleasant odour of geraniums. This characteristic counts as a flaw when tasting the wines.

The subtle fragrances of meadow flowers and fruit trees in blossom add to the elegance of dry white wines.

Violets, jasmine and iris

Certain floral aromas are common to both white and red wines. Violets are the best example of this. We find violet aromas combined with ripe apples in Mauzac de Gaillac grapes, for instance. Violets are also associated with wines based on Viognier and some white wines from the Savoie. In addition, the humble violet is among the aromas found in red wines based on Syrah and Cabernet Franc; likewise in those made from Négrette and especially Auxerrois. Even Pinot Noir can have an aroma of violets.

Dried flowers

Flowers in their natural state live for a season and then wither and die. Likewise, a wine with a floral bouquet will also fade. Poorly constituted wines eventually lose all bouquet, and with it their youthful charm. In more robust wines with the qualities to withstand several years of cellaring (alcoholic strength, acidity, concentration), the floral aromas develop into scents of dried flowers, infusions and herbal teas – the range of nuances can be quite diverse.

Assessing...
Fruit aromas in red wines

In the course of ripening, grapes acquire a distinctively fruity and especially complex bouquet as the sugar and acidity come into balance. The winegrower, however, must not allow them to ripen beyond peak maturity, or their fruitiness will seem heavy with notes of over-ripeness. A wine's development follows exactly the same pattern.

Red berries

- **Raspberry** is the most common aroma, found in grape varieties such as Pinot Noir, ripe Cabernet Franc, Syrah, Cinsaut and especially Gamay vinified by carbonic maceration.
- The aroma of **strawberries** is less common and often indicates riper grapes. Strawberry is an aroma characteristic of certain old wines at their peak.
- **Redcurrant** aromas, on the other hand, can suggests unripe grapes. In some red wines it also indicates a lack of sun.
- The aroma of **cherries** covers a broad category of scents. There are important distinctions within these aromas, ranging from the succulent, sharp scent of Bigarreau cherries to the fragrance of small black cherries that can be classified as 'black-skinned fruits' along with Burlat cherries (a larger, deep-red, firm-fleshed variant of Bigarreau), heart cherries and morellos. The aroma of cherries is often associated with the scent of the kernel of stone fruit. It may be classified as a scent of 'soft fruits'. Red cherries are beautifully expressed by Morgon wines; Chambertin and Volnay wines have a prominent scent of morellos.

Black-skinned fruits

The scent of black-skinned fruits is associated with a particular grape variety or very ripe grapes. Curiously, wines made from tannic grape varieties also express notes of black-skinned fruits.

- **Blackcurrant** is the black-skinned fruit aroma that is most often identified by tasters. It is expressed by many grape varieties, ranging from Pinot Noir and Cabernet Sauvignon, to Syrah, and even Fer-Servadou from Marcillac.
- The scent of **blackberries** is less common and is characteristic of Madiran wines that are based on low-yield, ripe Tannat grapes, and Savoie wines based on Mondeuse.
- **Little wild berries**, such as myrtle and blueberries are a sign of more rustic wines, or wines that lack maturity.

Cooked fruits

As the wine matures, the fresh fruit stage gives way to the cooked fruit stage; the fruit can be described as stewed or jammy. These aromas develop in cellared wines after several years of ageing, but they are also characteristic of certain young wines originating from the south of France. Wines based predominantly on Grenache, which is a rapidly developing variety, create a particularly strong impression of cooked fruits.

Carbonic maceration

This method of vinification gives supple, fruity wines with a lightly acidulous bouquet. The berries are macerated intact in tanks steeped in carbon dioxide. Thus fermentation cannot occur in the traditional manner due to the lack of oxygen. Instead, an intracellular enzymatic fermentation takes place within the intact grape and alcohol is produced, alongside aromatic compounds and colour. The grapes are then pressed and fermented in the usual manner.

Crystallised fruits

This aroma develops during maturation, between the fresh fruit and cooked fruit stage. It can also indicate great vintage wines from sunny regions. It may suggest raisins, desiccated grapes (*passerillé*) or sultanas. It is more typical of sweet white wines than red.

Dried fruit

Dried fruit aromas are generally characteristic of wines in the final stages of development. That said, the aromas of dried figs or hazelnuts expressed by great, cellared red wines, differ from the less noble notes of prunes and walnuts indicative of oxidation.

Soft stone-fruit

This category includes fruits such as cherries, plums, sloes, mirabelle plums, peaches and apricots. Only cherries and plums are noticeable in red wines, the rest are mainly associated with white wines. Plum aromas are quite rare, but can be found in some *vins doux naturels* (sweet wines) from the Midi.

Exotic fruits

The aroma of bananas is characteristic of *primeur* (very young) wines (usually based on Gamay) that have undergone carbonic maceration with aromatic yeasts. It is currently fashionable and detectable in Beaujolais Nouveau, Gaillac and *primeur* wines from Touraine.

Assessing...
Aromas of aged red wine

Bottle-ageing encourages predominantly animal-like, spicy, sometimes roasted scents. Where these aromas endure and are not destroyed by the airing or decanting processes, they go on to form part of the aromatic signature of the wine

Animal aromas

The way these aromas develop with age varies from one wine to another. The best examples of this can be found in Châteauneuf-du-Pape wines based on Grenache, supported by Syrah and Mourvèdre. These wines develop unevenly, their initially fruity bouquet giving way to often excessive animal aromas. With a little patience, however, the wine's fruity personality returns, combined with well-blended meaty, spicy notes.

• An aroma of leather indicates the start of the bouquet's development. At first discreet, it can become a distinctive mark of quality in old red wines. An aged St-Estèphe or Chambertin, while poles apart in many respects, do occasionally express the same kind of leathery scent.

• Aromas of fresh meat, and especially meat juices, greatly enhance the taste of a wine as they are usually echoed on the palate. Next to develop are more aggressive nuances, including the sweaty aromas that are associated

with some old red wines but only tolerable in small doses. Notes of rich game or meat stew, on the other hand, are approved of; some people delight in these aromas and rank the wines in question in the 'hunting' category, while others find them quite off-putting. Many of these wines possess a powerful bouquet that is not to everybody's taste, especially great Châteauneuf-du-Pape and the wines of Bandol, Hermitage, Pomerol, Pauillac, Madiran and Fitou. Animal aromas probably develop fastest of all in the wines that are based on Mourvèdre. If they are too strong, however, it is regarded as a serious flaw indicating over-reduction, or that the wine has suffered an attack from bacteria. To sum up, on their own, animal aromas, like most other scents, are off-putting and make the wine seem unbalanced, but when present in smaller doses, especially when well-integrated into the bouquet, they can benefit the wine greatly by adding to it's complexity.

Toasty, roasted, grilled aromas

These have various origins but are principally derived from tannins (grape and cask tannins) and are not unrelated to the ripeness of the harvest. The first indications of these aromas are scents of smokiness, smoked meat and tobacco smoke, followed by roasting/cooking nuances. They are associated with great tannic, oak-aged reds with the ability to age for several years. Such aromas can seem harsh if expressed alone, but when they are combined with scents of black-skinned fruits and game, they can add character to such long-lived wines. Also in this category are notes of roasting coffee and cocoa beans, which add body to old wines. They are prominent in Banyuls and Maury *vins doux naturels* and are characteristic of dry wines based on ripe Grenache and Syrah. Merlot often imparts chocolatey nuances to Pomerol wines.

Spicy aromas

Spicy aromas enliven meaty, roasted notes. The powerful scent of vanilla in young wines gradually makes way for aromas of cinnamon, nutmeg and cloves. Certain wines from the south of France reveal strong scents of herbs, including thyme, bay, oregano, savory and rosemary. Syrah wines from the great *terroirs* express scents of pepper and liquorice. And truffle, poised midway between vegetal and spicy aromas, can be picked up in very mature wines from Pomerol, Cahors or Bandol.

Animal aromas mark a wine just beginning to develop in bouquet and complexity. They merge with the toasty notes that remain from cask-maturation.

Well-aged Médoc and Cahors, and wines from the northern Rhône Valley, have a characteristic aroma of truffles.

A s s e s s i n g ...
The palate

asting a wine on the palate is above all a question of appreciating the synthesis of flavours. One must also appraise the balance of the wine's structure, distinguishing the attack, the mid-palate and the finish, discerning the elementary flavours, tannins and alcoholic warmth of the wine. This is the essence of the art of winetasting.

Taste

The traditional approach to tasting on the palate is to identify four elementary flavours: sweet, salty, acid and bitter. This is regarded as an oversimplification these days, but it remains useful for teaching purposes. Until the end of the 20th century, it was usual to distinguish specific zones on the tongue that could detect these elementary flavours: sweetness at the tip of the tongue, saltiness on the anterior sides, acidity on the posterior sides and bitterness at the back of the tongue. The latest scientific findings show that specific taste buds are, in fact, distributed all over the tongue but that bitterness is often only discernible on swallowing the wine, when the liquid hits the back of the tongue.

• The **olfactory sensations** are received by the retro-nasal route (**see p.31**). When the aromas reach mouth temperature, they are more intense than those received by the direct route. This brings out the less volatile elements in the bouquet. These 'flavours on the palate' are important. Far from being simple, fundamental flavours, they are the signature of the wine's taste.

• The **tactile sensation**: When tasting a red wine, the tannins (or their astringency, to be precise) give an indication of the wine's grain, weave and texture. This sensation is directly linked to the fluidity and viscosity of the saliva: excessive tannins make the mouth dry.

• The **thermal sensation** depends on the temperature of the wine but can be affected by the alcohol content which, if excessive, makes the wine seem warm.

TASTING BRIEF
Elementary flavours

Try to identify the elementary flavours in simple solutions tasted 'blind'. Practise this exercise in two stages comparing each solution with a plain glass of water. You can repeat the same exercise with the glasses in a different order.

1. Identification

Identify moderately concentrated solutions of the following substances mixed with water:

SALTY TASTE: 2 grams/litre cooking salt;

ACID TASTE: 1 gram/litre tartaric acid, or juice of half a lemon;

SWEET TASTE: 5 grams/litre sugar;

BITTER TASTE: 2 mg/litre quinine sulphate (available from chemists).

2. Noticing thresholds:
Prepare increasingly concentrated salty, acid, sweet and bitter solutions (stepping up the concentrations at the rates shown below). Now taste the glasses 'blind' in order. Note down the glass that gives you the impression of a taste (*perception threshold*) and the glass that allows you to identify the taste (*identification threshold*). Practise this exercise with a group of friends and you will discover huge variations in sensitivity to taste from one person to another. Some people genuinely prefer coffee without sugar, whatever the state of their waistline.

SALTY SOLUTION: 0.2, 0.4, 0.7, 1.5 and 3 grams/litre cooking salt.

ACID SOLUTION: 0.006, 0.12, 0.25, 0.5 and 1 gram/litre tartaric acid.

SWEET SOLUTION: 1, 2, 4, 6 and 8 grams/litre sugar.

BITTER SOLUTION: 0.6, 1.2, 2, 2.5, 4, 5 and 6mg/litre quinine sulphate.

Balance

A wine's balance depends on the relationship between its different chemical constituents.

• **The balance of flavours:** Wine contains sweet substances, acids, tannins and various salts. These elements come together in the mouth, each one adding to the qualities of the others and supporting them. In other cases, they may oppose and neutralise one another. A wine's harmony is essentially derived from the balance between the sweet tastes on the one hand and the acid, bitter tastes on the other. This is true of all wines including dry wines, because alcohol has a distinctly soft, sweet flavour of its own. Sugar counterbalances acidity as well as bitterness. It also influences the tannins in the wine by momentarily delaying the perception of astringency on the palate.

• **The balance between flavour and aroma**

For the taster, this is the most important balance. The brain analyses and brings together the flavours perceived on the palate and the aromas detected on the nose. The aromatic quality on the palate adds to the sense of balance and pleasure. The taster always explores the balance between two major aromatic components: fruit and… everything else. Fruit aromas are among the primary grape aromas modified by fermentation. Depending on their importance and nature, the other aromatic families compete with the fruit (a very

tannic wine, for instance, will stifle its fruit) or harmonise with it, creating a synergy that can last indefinitely. Some of the greatest wines are remarkable for the way their fruit content persists and evolves throughout its life, usually moving from white-fleshed or red fruits to cooked or soft fruits, or prunes.

The balance of white wines

• **Dry white wines**

The balance of a dry white wine is easier to understand because it is composed of just two elements: acidity and alcohol. Every white wine should be appraised on these two criteria. In graphic terms, they can be charted as two perpendicular axes (see below). The wine is represented by a point on the graph. If it sits near where the two axes cross, it is balanced.

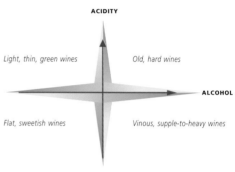

• **Sweet white wines**

The residual sugar in these wines affects their balance. It can be proved that the higher the sugar content, the more alcohol a wine should contain to remain harmonious and to avoid developing cloying notes. But some sweet German wines seem to defy this rule by being low in alcohol and rich in sugar, yet light and almost airy, thanks to their high acidity. For the same reason, a Jurançon or Coteaux-du-Layon wine will always be a much livelier wine than a Sauternes.

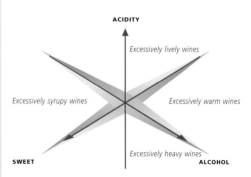

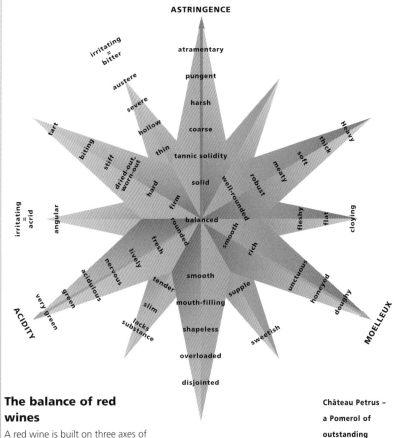

ASTRINGENCE

atramentary

pungent

harsh

coarse

irritating = bitter

austere

severe

hollow

thin

tannic solidity

Heavy

thick

soft

meaty

tart

biting

stiff

dried-out, worn-out

hard

solid

firm

well-rounded

robust

rich

cloying

flat

fleshy

irritating = acrid

angular

balanced

rounded

fresh

smooth

unctuous

MOELLEUX

lively

nervous

smooth

supple

honeyed

doughy

acidulous

tender

green

very green

ACIDITY

slim

lacks substance

mouth-filling

shapeless

sweetish

overloaded

disjointed

The balance of red wines

A red wine is built on three axes of balance: **acidity** and **sweetness,** as for white wines, plus **astringency** which arises from the tannin content. Red wine derives the majority of its sweetness from alcoholic strength which balances the combined effect of the acidity and astringency. High acidity must be equally balanced by high alcohol. High tannin content must be balanced by relatively low acidity and high alcohol. Conversely, a wine that is equally low in acidity and tannins needs very little alcohol for it to achieve a good balance.

Château Petrus – a Pomerol of outstanding balance.

Alcoholic warmth

Prepare increasingly concentrated solutions of water and pure alcohol, ranging from 8–20 per cent, for instance. Note the sensation of heat and the *moelleux*, sugary impression created by the alcohol (**see p.11**).

Sweetness

Start by comparing a glass of pure water with a solution of 10grams/litre glycerine. Note the difference between the rich and viscous effect on the palate and the sensation of sweetness due to the glycerol. Now add 15 per cent alcohol: the *moelleux* impression is greater. Lastly, add 10 grams sugar: the *moelleux* impression is at its strongest.

Astringency

Many foods have an astringent quality that causes the insides of the mouth to pucker. Good examples are globe artichokes, aubergines, some pears and plums, and raw chestnuts. Prepare a solution containing 0.5 grams/litre oenological tannins. Note the impression of dryness in the mouth and the structure of the solution. Increase the concentration to 1 gram/litre and you will notice the bitter sensation from the tannins.

Stages in analysis

1. Bring a small quantity of wine to mouth temperature then inhale briefly to release the aromas into the mouth. Your first impression is of a sweet, pleasant taste. These first few seconds of a tasting are known as the **attack**.

2. Roll the wine around the mouth for some ten seconds and notice how the aromas develop. At the same time, observe the temperature, the viscosity and, where relevant, the carbon dioxide and astringency of the wine. As your impressions grow increasingly complex, they reveal relationships that allow you to appreciate the wine's harmony and volume. This stage of the tasting is known as the **mid-palate.**

3. The **finish** tells you everything about a wine's structure, which should be firm but never aggressive or rough (when tasting red wines, the finish is always dominated by tannins). The vinous vapours in the mouth reflect the flavours on the palate. When tasting a great wine, the sensations persist long after you have spat out or swallowed the wine. A wine with substantial aromatic persistence is said to be 'long on the palate'. This persistence is measurable in *caudalies* (or seconds, **see** p.51) and is used to establish quality in wines.

Assessing...
Aromatic persistence

It takes years of practice to be able to truly appraise a wine's aromatic persistence, or length on the palate. Mastering this is one of the hardest aspects of tasting, but it is one of the most important skills when judging a wine.

The aromatic signature

Each stage of tasting a wine – visual, on the nose and on the palate – is focused on a physical aspect of the wine: its appearance, bouquet or taste. Length on the palate, however, is an important non-physical side to the wine, which is appraised after swallowing or spitting the wine out. This ephemeral power of expression singles wine out from other gustatory products, and is its personal signature.

The sum of the impressions

'*Un soir l'âme du vin dansait dans les bouteilles,*' wrote Baudelaire. ('One night the bottles were alive with the soul of wine.') Is it true that the soul of wine is only revealed after the curtain has fallen, as the artist makes his final exit? Length on the palate, or aromatic persistence, retentivity, aftertaste or finish, is in fact the sum of several impressions which, for simplicity's sake, we will describe here as *aromatic persistence* (AP), *structural length* or *aftertaste*.

To distinguish aromatic persistence, compare wines of different styles: the greatest wines will persist on the palate for more than ten *caudalies* and will 'open like a peacock's tail' (see p.51).

Persistence

Intense aromatic persistence means the continuation of the aromatic sensations on the palate. The heaviest, least volatile aromas usually leave the most lasting impression, while the lightest aromas are the first ones to disappear. The richer the flavours on the palate, and the denser and more full-bodied the wine, the better it will coat the mucous membranes of the palate and prolong the stimulation of the senses. Recording these impressions is therefore essential, as it allows the taster to establish a direct link between a sensory assessment and the quality of the wine.

Before swallowing the wine, and having made a note of its balance, fill your mind with its bouquet and focus on the most intense aroma. Try to remain focused on it after swallowing or spitting out the wine, and do not allow yourself to be distracted by other impressions. Note when that aroma disappears. The interval between the disappearance of the wine itself and the disappearance of the aroma can be measured in *caudalies* (from the Latin *cauda* meaning tail) or seconds. A wine of exceptional length is said by tasters to 'open like a peacock's tail'.

TASTING BRIEF

Compare an ordinary white table wine with an AOC (*Appellation d'Origine Contrôlée*) wine based on an aromatic grape variety like Sauvignon Blanc from Sancerre. The table wine has virtually no aromatic persistence whereas the Sancerre, depending on its quality, may have a length on the palate of five to eight *caudalies*. If you compare a red table wine with a Bordeaux Cru Bougeois, the first possesses a length on the palate of no more than two *caudalies*, but the Bordeaux reveals a greater aromatic persistence centred on red berries and spices. Compare the same Cru Bourgeois with a Premier Cru or Cru Classé. The aroma of the finish is the same in both cases but the cru classé is longer on the palate. Normally, the hierarchy of wines is maintained. That said, some exceptional Crus Bourgeois can far outrank disappointing Crus Classés.

Structural length

Appreciating aromatic persistence would be a straightforward process if other impressions did not get in the way. To understand the problem, try tasting a glass of household vinegar (a few drops will suffice). You will notice that the impression of pungent acidity remains on the palate long after the liquid itself has been spat out. Vinegar's length on the palate is derived solely from its acidity, devoid of any pleasant flavours. This is known as the structural length, or aftertaste, and ceases when salivation returns to normal. In the case of wine, however, the impressions produced by the acidity, alcoholic warmth, tannic astringency, bitterness and even sugar content can all persist on the palate, but play no part in the notion of quality. Excessive alcohol or tannins may well dominate the palate, but they are not the sign of a 'long' wine; only a wine with aromatic persistence can qualify as 'long'. Quality tannins are a vital ingredient of red wines; ripe tannins impart pleasantly lasting flavours which reinforce aromatic persistence, but green, bitter, vegetal or excessively wooded tannins destroy aromatic persistence. A wine that is unbalanced on the palate will never rank as a wine with length.

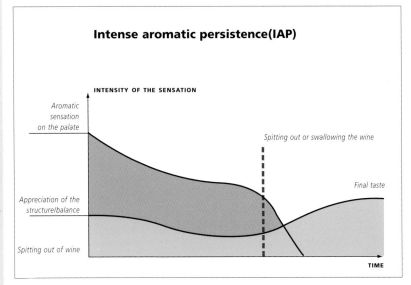

Assessing...
Faults in wine

Each of the different stages of tasting – eye, nose, palate – reveal how the wine was created and the way in which it has aged in the bottle. Not all wines emerge unscathed from the process, as you will discover when you come to taste them.

Eye

The eye of a wine does not lie. *Casses* (literally 'breakages') caused by precipitation of colouring material will make the wine cloudy. They are named after the element that causes the precipitation: copper, iron and protein. Most of the copper, ferric (iron) and proteic *casses* that used to destroy the wine's fragile colloidal balance have now been eliminated. Flaws in limidity and radiance are quite rare

The first test is to assess the wine's limpidity, which should be perfectly clear. Some old wines may throw a deposit but this has no effect on their quality.

these days. What remains are visual defects of a different nature, due mainly to a lack of pigmentation. This, in turn, could be because of excessive yields, insufficient ripeness or, perhaps, because the vinification was hurried as there were not enough tanks to cater for an abundant harvest. The colour of the wine, therefore, is an accurate way of judging a wine's development. Occasionally the fault may lie with the wine's constitution or its storage conditions once bottled. An overheated cellar, or wide fluctuations in temperature, can accelerate ageing, causing a wine to turn prematurely *tuilé* (reddish-brown or yellowish).

Nose

Flaws on the nose are more common and are usually caused by faults in the vinification and maturing processes, although unripe grapes, or a crop spoiled by grey rot, can also be to blame for this. Volatile acidity, once the scourge of even the greatest wines, is now little more than a bad

A flawless wine...

Paradoxically, a flawless wine is not necessarily a quality wine, however, it may well be a dull one. A rigidly technological approach has the ability to strip a wine of all its soul and reduce it to little more than a food. Eliminating unpleasant flavours or abnormal odours in wine is certainly a necessary process, but the procedures used should not purge the wine of all of its original character.

Sediment

When the sommelier presents a bottle of wine with sediment at the bottom, the customer is not impressed. Sediment is not sugar, however, but simply crystals of tartar in young wines, or pigments and tannins in old wines. It is perfectly normal and has no effect on the taste of the wine, provided it is carefully eliminated by decanting. Indeed, a total lack of sediment can be a worrying sign, suggesting that the wine has been treated to prevent sediment deposits.

memory and volatile wines are a thing of the past. The main defects these days are related to oxidation: too little results in *reduction odours*; too much leads to a bouquet dominated by *oxidation odours*. Poor maturation conditions remain a frequent cause of mouldy, stagnant-smelling wines; however, these are not to be confused with a corked taint.

Recently, a new problem has emerged: some products used to treat timber frameworks and wooden storage palettes,especially ethyl phenols, have a tendency to seep into the woodwork and may then contaminate the wine.

The only solution is to discard the palettes, or rebuild the winery. Some of these olfactory defects can be improved by airing and decanting. Others, sadly, cannot be redeemed.

Corked wines

When a wine smells or tastes of mould or old casks, it is described as 'corked' and is not fit for drinking. The defect only becomes apparent when the bottle is opened and it is due either to a mouldy cork or to the products that were used to treat it. Practise distinguishing between an authentic, ligneous, vegetal taste of cork and an unpleasant corked odour by comparing the smell of a healthy cork and a mouldy one. Every wine, however great, is at risk of being corked.

Palate

Faults on the palate upset the balance of the wine in one way or another. An excessively alcoholic wine may be the product of over-ripe grapes, but in most cases the fault lies with *chaptalisation*. Named after the chemist Chaptal, chaptalisation is the addition of sugar to the must to increase the alcohol content in the finished wine. The quantity of sugar added is strictly regulated depending on the region and the country, but despite these precautions, chaptalisation is often abused and remains a common cause of imbalance.

Overly high acidity is usually attributable to an under-ripe crop. Excess tannins are also due to a lack of ripeness, over-extraction during vinification or abnormally long periods in wood. Too little acidity, on the other hand, can lead to an absence of warmth, liveliness and structure, or to wines lacking in harmony and balance.

Mouldy corks give the wine an unpleasant vegetal odour; it is then described as 'corked'.

Tasting...
White wines

The approach to tasting white wines is fairly simple, as balance depends on just two factors: acidity and the alcohol-*moelleux* (mellow sweetness, **see p.11**) combination. White wines may be made for early drinking, in which case they feature primary, varietal or yeasty aromas (indicating recent fermentation). Others are destined for prolonged ageing in bottle. Vinification techniques vary accordingly.

Eye

• A white wine should look limpid and bright. Its natural clarity and translucence make any impurity, mistiness or colloidal particles readily visible. Sometimes a delicate bubble of gas rises to the surface, indicating a slight gasiness.

• The meniscus especially should be radiantly bright and completely free of floating particles.

• The intensity of pigmentation varies from one white wine to another depending on the grape variety, and more especially on the pressing and vinification techniques. Modern, state-of-the-art technology tends to produce dry, very pale, almost colourless white wines. More deeply coloured wines may have been fermented in cask. Very young white wines contain elements of blue that give them green reflections. Their colours range from lemon-yellow or yellow-green to straw-yellow. With advancing age, elements of brown introduce more golden notes of buttercup, topaz and old gold. These brown elements become dominant in very old wines – at the end of their lives they take on the russet, amber, brown or mahogany tones of advanced maderisation.

Nose

A white wine should be aromatic above all, so note the intensity of the nose: low to intense, discreet to developed, moderate to fragrant. An expressive nose indicates good intensity and a range of complex aromas. Study the nose in general:

Ugni Blanc (left) is a rather neutral grape variety; Gewürztraminer (below) is rich in aromatic potential.

The expression of the grape variety

Some varieties, such as Muscat, Sauvignon Blanc, Riesling and Gewürztraminer produce grapes with strong, aromatic potential. Traditional, simple vinification methods are sufficient to express their powerful aromas. Other varieties, such as Chardonnay and Marsanne, are less rich in varietal aromas, although their skins contain many potential aromatic elements which will only be fully revealed after the processes of fermentation and maturation have occurred. Such grape varieties are often used to make white wines suitable for ageing. More neutral grape varieties, such as Ugni Blanc, rely more heavily on technology to produce wine whose only merit is a bouquet marked by aromas of fermentation.

finesse, harmony and complexity of aroma. Then analyse it in detail to identify each scent or, failing that, each family of aromas.

Palate

There are two axes to the tasting of a white wine: acidity and the sensation of sweetness.

• Acidity contributes crispness and makes the wine refreshing. Carbon dioxide reinforces that impression and creates a prickly sensation on the tongue in the case of wines that are *perlant* or *moustillant* (slightly sparkling). The wine may be described as *lively, nervy, crisp* or *fresh*. The acidity should not be too pronounced, however, or the wine will be *green, hard, biting* or even

The effect of ripeness on grape expression

Unripe grapes possess strongly varietal characteristics plus herbaceous notes. Wines they produce must be consumed when young and fresh. Ripe grapes of the same variety release fruitier aromas that develop more complex nuances after vinification. Over-ripening 'burns' aromas, allowing for the characteristic bouquet of grapes after *passerillage* (heat-induced or partial drying).

Vinification techniques

Whether a white wine is for early drinking or laying down, care must be taken not to crush the grapes while picking and transporting them to the winery. There, they must be pressed as gently as possible, then clarified. Vinification methods vary depending on the finished wine: white wines for early drinking are usually matured in tanks while maturation in casks is generally reserved for wines for laying down.

• Yeast

Few white wines are made using naturally-occurring yeasts. These 'aromatic' or 'ambient' yeasts can enhance the flavours and traits of a wine, and are distinct from the more neutral, cultured yeasts that preserve the inherent qualities of the grapes.

• Vinification temperature

Wines vinified at very low temperatures have prominently yeasty aromas with a bouquet dominated by aromas of fermentation and amylase. Vinification

at higher temperatures produces more authentic (although perhaps less commercial) wines with the characteristics of the grape variety.

• Malolactic fermentation

This is usually avoided when the youthful characteristics of the wine are intended to be preserved.

tart and *stiff*. A wine with too little acidity, on the other hand, will seem *flat, flabby, flaccid* and *bland*.

• White wines that have undergone malolactic fermentation have less acidity and none of the tart properties associated with malic acid. But their range of aromas is modified in the process. Examples are white Burgundies, Swiss wines and some Champagnes.

• In dry white wines, the sensation of sweetness (*moelleux*) is created by the alcohol, glycerol and rare traces of residual sugar. The wine may be described as *agreeable, supple, soft, smooth, oily* or *suave*. It is a question of balancing two opposing tendencies. Judge the balance from the moment of attack, then as the aromas develop, then at the finish; it all depends on the richness of the aromas perceived by the retro-nasal route and revealed on the palate when the wine reaches mouth temperature. Once again, the type of balance will depend on the wine. Do not expect the same acidity to be present in a white Côtes-du-Rhône as in a Jurançon. The notion of dryness itself varies with the country. French dry white wines contain very little residual sugar – less than 2 grams/litre. German 'dry' white wines, on the other hand, are much higher in sugar content, masking high acidity levels. This combination of sugar and high acidity gives these wines an *acidulous* quality. It is easier to judge the length of a white wine than a red wine, as the impression of length is not concealed by tannins.

Maceration with skin contact (*macération pelliculaire*)

Grape skins contain potential aromatic elements that can be released by prolonged contact with the must prior to fermentation. In a *macération pelliculaire* the grapes are lightly crushed and left to macerate in the cold must for several hours.

Maturation on the lees
(l'élevage sur lies)

The viscous deposits remaining at the bottom of the tank or barrel after vinification are called 'lees'. The 'gross lees' that might spoil the finished wine are removed by *racking*. The fine lees, on the other hand, can be left in contact with the wine during the maturation process. This occurs in Muscadet-de-Sèvre-et-Maine Sur Lie and Gros Plant du Pays Nantais. Vinification may include regularly stirring the wines in the casks to keep the lees in suspension (*bâtonnage*). This technique is traditionally used to reinforce the richness and complexity of Burgundy wines.

After swallowing or spitting out the wine, simply close your eyes and then allow the wine to 'live' on the palate – as though you were tasting the wine 'virtually'.

The effect of
maturing on the lees

Vinification on the lees aims to preserve a wine's primary fruit aromas (see p.34) and its freshness while maintaining the carbon dioxide (see p.11) which adds a certain liveliness.

Aromatic series of white wines

Series	Aromas	Wines
Vegetal	• Fresh grass, hay, green leaves • Herbal infusions, herb tea • Box, ivy, fern • Tea, tobacco, dead leaves • Undergrowth, mushrooms	• Young wines, early harvested grapes • Chardonnay • Sauvignon Blanc • Oak-aged wines • Old wines
Aromatic vegetal	• Mint, thyme, anise, truffles	• Rolle, Clairette, wines from the south of France

Floral	• Acacia, dog rose, honeysuckle
	• Violets, iris, hawthorn, roses,
	  heather, broom
		• Chardonnay
		• Aromatic grape varieties: Riesling,
		  Gewürztraminer, Viognier

Fruit
- white-fleshed
  fruits
- citrus
 	
- exotic fruits
 	
- dried fruits
	
	• Apples, peaches, pears
	• Melon, apricots
	• Grapefruit, lemons, oranges,
	  citrus peel, citron
	• Lychees, pineapple, mango
	• Quince
	• Walnuts, hazelnuts, almonds
		
		• Mauzac, Marsanne, Sémillon
		• Sweet wines, Muscat
		• Sauvignon Blanc, sweet wines
		
		• Manseng, Sauvignon Blanc
		• Chenin, sweet wines
		• Aged Chardonnay, Marsanne,
		  Jura wines

Spicy	• Cinnamon, vanilla, cloves	• Cask-aged wines
Wooded and balsamic	• Oak, balsa, cedar, pine, resin, eucalyptus	• Cask-aged wines
Empyreumatic	• Smoked, roasted, tobacco	• Cask-aged wines
Mineral	• Gunflint, naphtha, pencil lead	• Sauvignon Blanc, Riesling

Fermentation	• Yeast, white bread (dough only),
	  brioche, butter, yoghurt,
	  boiled sweets, varnish
		• Wines matured on lees,
		  Champagne, recent malolactic
		  fermentation, technological wines

Chemical	• Sulphur • Alcohol, rotten eggs • Iodine	• Excessive sulphur dioxide • Reduction • Manzanilla

Honey-confectionery	• Honey, praline, marzipan,
	  beeswax, polish
		• Sweet and *liquoreux* wines,
		  old wines

Tasting...
Young white wines

Young white wines indulge the taste buds with their freshness, fruitiness and their balance of *moelleux* and acidity. These are accessible, easy-drinking wines, and they highlight the basic elements of tasting.

Eye

White wines are generally pale-coloured with slight variations according to fashion – some of the whites produced in the past were virtually colourless. Winemakers these days tend to be more sensible, producing young, straw-coloured whites characterised by green highlights of different levels of intensity.

Nose

Young white wines can reveal aromas from all major aromatic families.

Vegetal series: fresh grass, freshly cut hay, fern, blackcurrant buds, boxwood. Some wines express scents of herbal infusions such as lime blossom and verbena, or of aromatic plants such as anise, lavender and fennel.

Floral series: acacia, honeysuckle, roses, carnations, wild flowers, broom, lime blossom, citronella, jasmine.

Fruit series: dominated by scents of white-fleshed fruits (apples, pears, white peaches, apricot, quince).

Fermentation series: bananas, yeast, acid drops, white bread (dough only), brioche.

Spicy series (to a lesser extent).

Palate

White wines can be divided into two categories depending on their balance. Northern vineyards tend to produce white wines that are fairly high in acidity, with a natural freshness that accentuates their fruity bouquet. The finish is extremely refreshing. Winemakers sometimes restore harmony, either by retaining some residual sugar, as in Alsace, or by using malolactic fermentation methods (**see** p.58), as in Burgundy. Wines from southern regions occasionally lack acidity. As they are somewhat softer and less refreshing, their merit lies in their richness and volume on the palate. They are perfectly suited to the spicy dishes favoured in the region. Being matured on the lees, these wines may have a slightly pearly quality.

White wines for early drinking

France: Gaillac, wines from Provence and the Languedoc, Côtes-du-Rhône, Condrieu, Alsace-Sylvaner, Alsace-Pinot Blanc.

South Africa: Chardonnay.

Germany and Austria: Silvaner, Riesling Kabinett, Pinot Blanc.

California: Chardonnay.

Chile: Chardonnay.

Spain: Rioja, Rias Baixas, Penedès.

Italy: Est! Est!! Est!!!, Orvieto, Soave, Veneto, Friuli, Frascati.

Luxembourg: Riesling.

New Zealand: Sauvignon Blanc.

Portugal: Vinho Verde.

Switzerland: Fendant du Valais.

Slovenia: Chardonnay.

Ukraine: Aligoté, Sauvignon Blanc.

Opposite: fresh grass, white fruits, flowers; young white wines express a profusion of vegetal aromas and floral. Alsace-Sylvaner is a dry, fruity wine to be drunk when young and fresh.

Tasting...
White wines for laying down

Good ageing ability is relatively rare in white wines, but those with sufficient strength and balance do improve with age, acquiring unique aromas and an overall complexity based on a harmonious blend of constituents.

Eye

The colour of a white wine develops fairly quickly with age, youthful green reflections gradually giving way to elements of gold. With time, the wines take on the full spectrum of golden tones ranging from pale gold to old gold, with occasional glints of copper.

Nose

The primary aromas of white wine slowly give way to a more complex bouquet; the varietal characteristics and aromas of fermentation also begin to fade, giving way finally to the aromas of ageing. It is interesting to note how these aromas evolve in terms of their series and nature. The aroma of roses noticeable in Gewürztraminer, for instance, develops first into a scent of faded roses then into the fragrance of dried flowers. The aroma of apricots develops from the scent of young fresh fruit into the fragrance of ripe apricots, then dried apricots.

The vegetal series is confined to notes of dried grass, tobacco,

Vinifying Burgundy: white wines are fermented in casks.

herbal infusions and dead leaves. The fruit series is based on dried bananas, walnuts, hazelnuts and roasted almonds, while the spicy series is most obvious, with notes of cinnamon, vanilla, nutmeg, amber and musk. It can also include hints

of truffle, the ultimate reward of a memorable tasting. The aroma that is common to all mature white wines, irrespective of their primary aromas, is a definite note of wax, or even polish.

The role of the cask

As they are devoid of tannins, white wines are at the mercy of oxidation and the other dangers that inevitably come with age. Their only protection against the rigours of time are strength, structure and especially acidity – their only defence against bacterial attack. The tannins that are contributed by the cask, however, can help to compensate for a natural lack of tannins in white wines. Cask maturation is a special process in which white wines undergo a lightly oxidative phase. The wine is then transferred to a reductive environment in the bottle where it commences life as a wine suitable for laying down.

Palate

Strong, concentrated, well-structured, lively wines will achieve a harmonious character with time. Generally speaking, white wines with the most pronounced acidity in their youth calm down with age. Some wines, though, grow increasingly acid and gaunt when they reach the limits of their ageing ability. In the same way, oxidation aromas should remain discreet and well integrated with the other aromatic elements in the wine. An aged white wine therefore walks something of a tightrope – the smallest provocation can tip the balance one way or the other.

Dry white wines with good ageing potential

• **Marsanne** and **Roussanne**
White Hermitage wines are among the French whites most capable of withstanding the test of time. They owe their ageing ability not to acidity – which is quite low – but to their strength and concentration. Marsanne wines are spicy and honeyed at first, growing beautifully complex with a range of dried fruit aromas.

• **Riesling**
These lively but tender wines know how to grow old gracefully. Their originally spicy, floral aromas gradually express that celebrated mineral nuance of petrol that should never be regarded as a defect.

• **Chenin**
Wines based on Chenin, especially Les Savennières from the Loire,

probably have the best ageing ability. Thanks to good underlying acidity (which can be unbalanced in youth) they survive ageing unmarked. As young wines they are not particularly aromatic, but with time they express a delicate bouquet of dried flowers, herb teas, dried fruits and honey.

• **Chardonnay**
Great white Burgundies also grow old gracefully. They are vinified and matured in casks, enriched by their lees and the aromas of the wood, and have the strength and vigour to withstand long ageing. With time, they acquire unmistakable aromas of dried fruits, almonds, hazelnuts, faded flowers and herbal infusions (lime blossom or verbena). Delicious honeyed notes come later, adding softness and roundness to one of the most thoroughbred of all bouquets.

• **Viognier**
These wines have little youthful liveliness and a slender structure but they are remarkably resistant, developing a harmonious range of dried fruit, wax, spice and tobacco aromas with time. The palate has prolonged roundness and meatiness. Condrieu, from the Rhône, reveals this to best effect.

• **Sauvignon Blanc** and **Sémillon**
Together, Sauvignon and Sémillon work wonders in dry white Graves wines, the Sémillon taking over from the Sauvignon as it loses it youthful exuberance with time. Maturity brings unmistakably honeyed, spicy notes that blend with the fruit of the Sauvignon.

As wines age, fresh vegetal notes take on nuances of tobacco and undergrowth.

Tasting...
Red wines

Tasting red wine can be a difficult exercise, but is richly rewarding in terms of colour, aroma, structure and velvety tannins. By following a few key steps, you will soon become familiar with red wine's characteristics, and will enjoy the process of analysis.

Opposite: tasting Châteauneuf-du-Pape

Eye

A wine's colour says something about its age, concentration and richness. First, consider the brightness and limpidity of the colour then inspect the meniscus by looking down into the glass. The surface of the wine should be shiny and free of any floating particles. Note the nuances of colour overlaying the overall colour around the edges of the glass. They are the first signs of development.

The intensity of colour may be *poor, light, clear, sustained, dark, deep* or *intense*. Poor intensity of colour, in a young Syrah or Cabernet Sauvignon, for instance, indicates a harvest washed out by heavy rain, excessive yields and short periods of tank fermentation. This is obviously a defect. The same intensity of colour in a Pinot Noir or Gamay, on the other hand, would be regarded as perfectly normal.

Young red wines display violetty shades with elements of blue. These fade with time to be replaced by yellow tints. The wines then take on violet, brick-red and eventually brown tones (**see p.29**). Brown shades indicate a wine of advanced years, or one that has been stored poorly. Lastly, examine the traces of wine (tears) that remain on the inside of the glass. These are indications of alcohol, glycerol and residual sugar content.

Nose

Having noted the most obvious aromas, give the glass a good swirl to aerate the wine and flush out hidden aromas. Begin by studying the aromatic intensity of the bouquet. A wine is said to be closed when the aromatic expression is reticent. This can be a problem with some great red wines although fortunately it is usually only a passing phase.

Next, analyse the different aromatic elements. Lastly, note how the nose develops with time by smelling the bouquet once again at the end of the tasting.

Vinification techniques

The method of vinification has a powerful effect on the character of red wines, especially young ones.

• **De-stemming**
This refers to the total or partial separation of the grapes from the stems. Because stem tannins are usually more herbaceous than grape tannins, separating the grape bunches from the stems makes for a more supple wine. Retaining a certain proportion of stems can improve wines based on low tannin grape varieties, like Pinot Noir.

• **Crushing**
This process is used to burst the grapes or liberate the juice and bring it into contact with the grape skins. Crushing can be partial or total, and must be gentle enough not to break the skins or crush the pips. It is not used when the grapes are to undergo carbonic maceration.

• **Alcoholic fermentation**
The style of a wine depends on two factors: *temperature and the intensity and duration of extraction*.
– *Temperature*. Low temperatures bring out the fruity nature of the wine. Raising the temperature draws out the high anthocyanin levels (**see p.10**) and tannins required in wines for laying down.
– *Intensity and duration of extraction*. Extraction brings the juice into contact with the solid grape matter. Bordeaux wines undergo *remontage*: pumping must from the tank bottom to the top, over the cap of the pulp (*marc*). Burgundy wines undergo *pigeage*: submerging the cap into the must, once done by foot, now mechanically. Tannin concentration depends on the frequency of *remontage* or *pigeage*. The length of tank fermentation determines the intensity of tannic extraction.

• **First pressings and press wine**
The juice drawn off

Palate

There are three axes to the analysis of red wines: *acidity*, the *moelleux* sensation and tannins. Begin by examining the attack (your first impression of the wine on the palate), which might be fleeting or firm. Then study its development on the palate. Then the finish. Think of these three stages, or impressions, as the skeleton of the wine. To this will be added the flesh or solid matter – the substance, or body, of the wine. This substance develops flavours on the palate that are detected by the retro-nasal route. These may not be the same as those identified by the direct route when the wine on the palate reaches a temperature of 30°C (86°F) and releases its least volatile aromas. At each stage, examine the balance between the acid, the *moelleux* sensation and especially the

the tank is known as the first pressings (*vin de goutte*). Pulp is pressed to give press wine (*vin de presse*) which is deeper in colour, higher in tannins and more aggressive. Depending on the quality of the press wine, and how robust the winemaker wants the final wine to be, they may blend a proportion of press wine with the first pressings.

Sorting grapes at Château Clarke (Listrac-Médoc).

tannins. The tannins can create an almost tactile sensation on the tongue and the gums; they add astringency which, if too weak or too strong is regarded as a defect. Quality tannins, though, indicate a great red wine. You may detect relatively weak tannic strength with a dry texture or, on the other hand, impressive tannic strength with a delicate texture. Conditions favouring velvety tannins are: ripe grapes; carefully controlled extraction during vinification; and long, but not protracted, periods of maturation in quality oak. The *moelleux* sensation of a red wine is the combined effect of the alcohol and glycerine, and is always perceived as a good feature. In comparative tastings, alcoholic strength often determines a winning wine, to the detriment of the acid or tannic impressions that can assault an inexperienced or exhausted palate. Make no mistake, however: alcoholic strength may be seductive but it is never an element of finesse or balance. The so-called 'touch' of the wine on the other hand – that tactile sensation that acknowledges the ripeness of the tannins – is a key factor when distinguishing between red wines. Known in French as the *trame* (literally 'weave'), this sensation, together with length on the palate, makes it possible to truly judge the quality of red wines.

Length on the palate (a wine's aromatic persistence after it has been swallowed or spat out) is the lingering property of tasting. Make a note of its duration.

Series of aromas in red wines

Series	Aromas	Wines and grape varieties
Vegetal	• Blackcurrant buds • Peppers • Tobacco • Fungi • Truffles	• Syrah, Fer-Servadou • Cabernet Sauvignon • Cask-matured wines • Older wines • Pomerol, Cahor
Floral	• Roses, violets, peonies	• Young wines, Pinot Noir, Gamay
Fruit	• Soft fruits • Black-skinned fruits • Soft fruits (with stones) • Dried fruits	• Young wines • Wines made from very ripe grapes, southern wines, Syrah, Tannat, Mourvèdre • More developed wines, Pinot Noir • Indicates the start of oxidation
Spicy*	• Cinnamon, vanilla	• Cask-matured wines
Wooded*	• Oak, balsa, eucalyptus	• Cask-matured wines
Empyreumatic*	• Cocoa, toast	• Tannat, Grenache, Mourvèdre
Animal**	• Meat juices, leather, game	• Developed wines, Grenache

* These three series are present in cask-matured wines, and wines made from very ripe Syrah, Cabernet or Merlot grapes, and from Mourvèdre or Tannat grapes.
** Animal odours that disappear when the wine is aired indicate temporary reduction. A pronounced odour of venison is a defect.

Tasting...
Young red wines

A young red wine is marked by its youthful fruit and impetuous tannins. Depending on whether the wine is destined to be drunk at once or to be laid down, it is a source of immediate pleasure, or pleasure in store.

Eye

A young wine should appear limpid and bright, but the intensity of colour varies widely from one appellation to another, from light red for Beaujolais Nouveau to the deep tones of a young Côte-Rotie – the range is infinite. In their youth, red wines are dominated by elements of blue, even violet. The shade of red may be cherry, redcurrant or raspberry depending on the grape varieties used to blend the wine. There may even be nuances of crimson, blackcurrant, garnet, violet and ink. The meniscus rarely reveals any signs of development except in the case of a prematurely aged wine. The blue element is most visible around the rim of the meniscus.

Nose

• A young red wine still gives pride of place to its varietal aromas combined with the yeasty aromas of fermentation. Depending on the type of wine, the floral and fruit series are first to emerge – scents of peonies, violets and roses mingling with aromas of soft fruits such as redcurrants, cherries, strawberries, raspberries and morellos. Carbonic maceration (see p.43) produces aromas of isoamyl acetate such as acid drops or bananas.

• A red wine destined for long periods of cellaring presents quite different aromas. It may have little aromatic intensity, or the bouquet may be masked. Far from being a defect, this is an essential phase in the life of the wine. The range of aromas is sometimes enriched with notes of spice, balsam, liquorice or pepper. Because these wines are often cask-matured, the bouquet is overlaid with aromas of wood, vanilla, cedar and toast.

Palate

• A wine that is light on the palate is not necessarily a watery wine. But it should have a foundation of fruit and suppleness, with an honest attack creating an immediate impression of characteristic fruitiness. The balance of the wine should favour freshness and ripe substance but alcoholic strength should remain discreet – although this is not always the case with many young wines. The tannins should be ripe, supple and already smooth. Some styles of wine have a certain fullness, adding a pleasant, rustic element.

• When tasted young, wines for laying down show a strong tannic framework, dense substance and fruit. Their impressive, sometimes severe, structure is especially noticeable. These wines need more time to mature.

Opposite: tasting Bourgeuil

Red wines for early drinking

France: Beaujolais, Loire wines, young Côtes-du-Rhône wines, Languedoc wines, Alsace-Pinot Noir, regional appellation Burgundies.
Spain: Rioja Joven, Jumilla, La Mancha.
Italy: Bardolino, Valpolicella, Chianti, Alto Adige Merlot.
USA: Zinfandel, Gamay.
Chile and Argentina: Merlot.

Tasting...
Aged red wines

The tannins, acidity or structure of a very young wine often provide a good indication of its potential for ageing. But nothing can replace tasting experience. Only knowledge of a particular appellation, cru or estate can provide all the information that is needed to judge the cellaring potential of a wine.

Eye

The colour of the wine is first dominated by shades of blue (such as violet and purple). These are gradually replaced by more orange tones. As the colour becomes less intense, ruby will change first to vermilion then to cherry, *tuilé* (reddish-brown or yellowish), brick-red, and a pale rosé before acquiring the distinctive mahogany hue that is characteristic of old wines when they have reached the peak of their colour development.

Nose

An aged wine has distinctively complex aromas: by this stage it has developed a bouquet. From the moment of bottling, the wine then enters a reductive phase. This has a progressive effect on the aromas. First, the empyreumatic series becomes noticeable. Next comes the animal series, which is typical of wines that have been aged in the bottle: leather then meaty notes, followed by scents of game and (often pungent)

notes of venison. In some wines this gamey phase diminishes with age and the wine then returns to fruity notes. Some wines develop aromas that are remniscent of mushrooms, undergrowth and humus, but these should remain discreet. A generous aroma of truffles, however, is often pleasant and agreeable.

Palate

A very young red wine can often appear to be somewhat aggressive in structure. It draws its overall firmness from astringent tannins with impressive solidity and acidity – these should blend and mellow over the course of time. This is not always the case, however: some tannic or rustic wines can suddenly collapse without ever acquiring elegance. Powerful tannins with an already delicate tactile texture are the sure sign of a wine that is capable of impressive

Great red wines for laying down

Bordeaux: Médocs, Graves, St-Emilion Grand Cru, Pomerol.
Burgundy: Pommard, Vosne-Romanée, Gevrey-Chambertin, Corton, Volnay, Clos de Vougeot.
Australia: Shiraz, Penfolds Grange.
Spain: Rioja, Priorato, Ribera del Duero.
USA: Californian Cabernet Sauvignon.
Italy: Barolo, Barbaresco, Brunello di Montalcino, Recioto, Super Tuscans.

harmony. Its tannins will gradually condense and lose their dryness, to be replaced by a velvety structure, suppleness and finesse. This is the optimal phase of development and it tends to vary in duration depending on the wine. Eventually the structure grows thinner and the wine's acidity, alcohol and astringency become increasingly evident. Elements that once combined to form a harmonious blend now separate. When it reaches this stage, the wine is at the end of its life.

At their peak, great aged red wines are deeply coloured with shades of mahogany.

TASTING BRIEF

Tracing the development of a red wine for laying down

A red wine for laying down goes through several stages in its life. As a young wine, it is very open, especially if tasted in the cellar from the barrel or tank. It then falls victim to bottling: its aromas close and its fleshiness withers and grows flabby. Only the structure still reflects its former qualities. After one or two years, depending on the wine, the healing process begins: the wine withdraws into itself for a long period of reflection. Tasting a wine in this condition can be heartbreaking, like finding yourself in front of a padlocked door to which you have lost the key. Your only option is to wait for the wine to open up.

Tasting...
Rosé wines

Is it possible to have a serious rosé wine tasting? Or are these wines, neither red nor white, merely the quaffable accompaniment to simple dishes – a plate of traditional French *charcuterie*, for example? In fact, there are some astonishing rosé wines, with real style and personality, from a range of different wine regions worldwide.

Vinification techniques

There are two methods for making rosé wine, each of which produces wines of quite different character.

• The pressing method using red or pink-skinned grapes: this yields a pale juice which is then vinified as for white wine. The finished rosé obtained by this method is known as *vin gris*. Rosé wines created by pressing have similar aromas and flavours to those belonging to white wines.

• The *saignée* method: here, the grapes are vinified as for red wine until the winemaker decides that sufficient colour has been extracted. The tank is then 'bled' by running off the liquid from the solid matter (skins, seeds, etc.). The juice obtained continues to ferment as for white wine. This method produces a greater depth of colour, although the intensity tends to vary with each region. Rosé wines made by the *saignée* method have a certain tannic richness and appear more vinous than rosés made by the pressing method. They include a type of rosé wine that is known in French as '*d'une nuit*' (literally a 'one-night rosé'). With both of the methods described above, the juice is usually vinified at a low temperature to encourage the aromatic yeasts to bring out the full fruity potential of the must.

Tavel wines are limpid and pale pink in youth, acquiring nuances of pale gold then copper after a year's ageing.

Eye

The enticing shades of a rosé wine sharpen the taste buds almost as much as its aromas or flavours. Notice the strength of colour first: it should correspond to the type of wine. Too little intensity can be a defect in a wine from one appellation, but a positive quality in another. Too much intensity, making the wine pale red rather than rosé, can be misleading. As with white wine, once you have noted brightness and limpidity, try to define the particular shade of colour. There is a whole spectrum of pink modified by varying elements of blue on the one hand, or brown on the other. You can therefore find wines that range from pale grey to pale pink, plain pink, peony, cherry, raspberry, strawberry, antique pink, orange-pink, apricot, salmon, brick-red, russet and pale rosé. A Gamay rosé is more cherry-pink, a Cabernet rosé is raspberry pink and a Carignan rosé displays orange tones.

Tavel is dedicated to the production of rosé wines based on Grenache Noir, Cinsaut, Syrah and Mourvèdre.

Palate

A rosé wine should always be refreshing. Judge its balance from its liveliness and acidity, *moelleux* quality, richness and vinous strength. Consider the quality of the attack, which should be sound and aromatic: the wine should be immediately communicative. There should be detectable but balanced acidity. A rosé wine with too little acidity seems flat, heavy and brashly alcoholic. Too much acidity, on the other hand, makes the wine seem green and tart. The right acidity brings out the wine's fruity personality and overall appeal.

The sulphur dioxide question

Rosé wine has been known to cause headaches, which has a tendency to put people off drinking it. This is due to the high levels of sulphur dioxide (SO_2) that are added to prevent oxidation in poorly constituted or badly made rosé wines, or in wines that have been made from poor grapes.

However, the defect may not be noticeable at all if the rosé is served well chilled. Sulphur dioxide can be detected on the nose by its characteristically sulphurous odour. On the palate, it will cause a nasty prickly sensation at the back of the throat. Well-made rosés, however, contain only small amounts of sulphur dioxide and will cause no ill effects.

Nose

Rosé wine should always be aromatic. You will notice floral, fruit and vegetal aromas together with scents of fermentation and amylase. Wooded, balsamic and animal aromas are rarer occurrences. Spicy aromas however – especially peppery nuances – can be detected in rosés produced from Syrah grapes (e.g. Côtes-du-Rhône rosés). More mature rosés (such as Tavel) have a bouquet similar to that of red wines; empyreumatic notes that gradually make way for hints of cooked fruit and jam, then aromas of undergrowth and meaty scents which suggest that the wine is coming close to the end of its life.

Carbon dioxide content may enhance the wine's liveliness but it should never be too obvious. Note the intensity and persistence of the aromatic impression on the palate. It derives its body from the wine's relative tannic strength, which should be neither too heavy nor too robust. A light, aromatic rosé wine is best served as an aperitif or as an accompaniment to cold buffets. A more solidly structured rosé with richer tannins can be a nice accompaniment to meals.

Irouléguy rosé, from the sloping vineyards in the foothills of the Pyrenees, is a sound, aromatic raspberry-coloured wine with scents of wild flowers and light tannins. It is produced by the *saignée* method.

Series of aromas in rosé wines

Series	Aromas	Wines
Vegetal	• Blackcurrant blossom, pepper	• Cabernet rosé
Floral	• Orange blossom, hawthorn, peach blossom, vine blossom, peony, roses, lime flower, iris, violets, carnation, heather, broom, dried flowers	• Rosé wines made from Négrette or Pinot Noir
Fruit	• Cherry, redcurrant, blackcurrant • Strawberry, raspberry • Apricot, peach, pear, apple, fresh figs • Citrus, exotic fruits, fresh almonds	• Pinot Noir rosé • Rosés made from Cabernet Sauvignon, Tannat or Cinsaut • Grenache rosé • Rosé wine made from technological processes
Fermentation	• Yeast, acid drops	•Technologically made rosé wine
Spicy	• Pepper	• Rosé wine made from Syrah or Mourvèdre

Tasting...
Sweet wines

When you taste sweet wines, you understand the meaning of the French expression *'l'or du vin'* (the gold in wine). These radiant wines, with their exotic floral or fruit aromas and velvety textures, have an eternal, nectar-like quality.

Eye

A sweet wine has more depth and intensity of colour than a dry wine. It is also viscous and rich in tears. The colour is dominated by golden shades varying from pale gold, golden yellow or buttercup, to antique gold. As they begin to age, sweet wines will take on copper tones, followed by shades of amber, russet, fawn, brown and even mahogany, as can be found in bottles that date from the 19th century.

Nose

Wines that are produced from grapes affected by *Botrytis cinerea* (noble rot) have noticeable aromas of apricots, sweet spices, bread and praline. However, if the fungus does not develop in the right conditions, it leads to adulterated aromas of iodine and mushrooms, or notes of humus. When the fungus does not develop at all, such as can happen in very dry years, the aromas will acquire rich notes of jam or honey but the wines are less complex.

The sweet wines of Jurançon tend to be more vivacious than those from Sauternes thanks to the Petit Manseng grapes used.

Sweet wines have a complex bouquet dominated by scents of fruit, plus additional notes of great maturity. The predominant aroma in young sweet wines is that of crystallised citrus fruit, but floral notes such as orange blossom are also common. Next to develop are scents of exotic fruits (lychees, mangoes and pineapple, for example) and crystallised fruits (quince jelly, angelica). Botrytised Pinot Gris and Gewürztraminer grapes that are used to make *sélection de grains nobles* wines from Alsace contribute spicy notes of their own. In older wines, the bouquet is overlaid by empyreumatic (toast, caramel) and spicy aromas (vanilla, cinnamon, sometimes anise) with additional nuances of confectionery (honey, praline, marzipan). Aged sweet wines acquire hints of polish (beeswax) allied to mature spicy aromas and elegant nuances of *rancio*.

How sweet wine is made

Musts that are used to make dry wines contain approximately 200 grams/litre of sugar. Sweet and *liquoreux* wines require much sweeter grapes in which the sugar has been concentrated by allowing the grapes to become over-ripe. Part of the sugar in the grapes is converted into alcohol, but part of it remains in the wine as residual sugar. There are several different ways of obtaining the right concentrations of sugar concentrations, which can be as high as 350–400 grams/litre.

• *Botrytis cinerea*

Certain microclimates favour the development of *Botrytis cinerea*. Where the winegrower allows this mould to develop, it spreads its mycelium over thick-skinned grapes such as Sémillon and Chenin, perforating the skin and allowing the moisture to evaporate. This shrivels the grapes which lose their acidity but grow rich in sugar and acquire distinctive honeyed aromas. Botrytised grapes are picked in successive batches (from the same row, several times) as the mould gradually starts to spread. French wine regions that encourage *Botrytis cinerea* begin to the south of Bordeaux in Sauternes and extend into Monbazillac, the Loire Valley, Alsace and the Rhineland. Noble rot develops outside France in vineyards in central Europe, Austria, Bulgaria and Hungary.

• *Passerillage*

This refers to the partial drying or desiccation of the grapes. In regions with dry autumns, such as the Jurançon, the grapes are left to dry on their stalks. In the Jura the ripest, healthiest grapes are picked and then dried on frameworks of widely spaced wooden slats known locally as *claies*. The grapes were traditionally dried on beds of straw, but these days are hung to dry on wires in a well-aired space.

Botrytis cinerea spreads itself unevenly over the grape bunch. The grapes must then be picked by hand in successive batches as the mould spreads.

Palate

The balance of a sweet wine is often expressed in terms of alcohol content. A sweet wine with a balance of 14–4 has an alcoholic strength of 14 per cent abv plus a residual sugar content of 70 grams, which is equivalent to four degrees of alcohol. Too much alcohol makes the wine seem fiery; too much residual sugar makes it heavy and flabby. Fortunately, however, balance is maintained by acidity. The greater the level of acidity, the lighter and more harmonious the sweet wine will be. German wines, for example, are rich in sugar but have an almost airy quality, thanks to good acidity and modest alcohol levels. Barsac often has a pronounced liveliness which distinguishes it from Sauternes. Likewise Jurançon or Quarts-de-Chaume seem less sweet and more quaffable, because of the high levels of acidity provided by the Petit Manseng and Chenin grapes used. The palate of a sweet wine should also be judged in terms of complexity and smoothness. Sweet wines are complex, powerful and concentrated; they have all the necessary mouth-filling qualities. These are the longest wines, with powerful aromas that settle triumphantly on the palate, filling up all the space and ruling supreme at the finish.

Tasting...
Vins jaunes

*V*in jaune (literally 'yellow wine') is a French white wine made mainly in the Jura from a single grape variety, Savagnin, and matured below a veil of yeasts. Tasting requires an understanding of the vinification process, but even a beginner can appreciate its remarkable length.

Eye

Because it is matured in an oxidised environment, *vin jaune* begins life with the golden tones of an aged wine. These turn to shades of amber and antique gold, eventually acquiring a coppery hue. The name *vin jaune,* however, refers to the taste of the wine, not the colour.

Vin jaune from the Jura is matured for six years and three months beneath a film of yeasts.

Maturation *sous voile*

Savagnin grapes from the Jura generally have an alcohol content of at least 13 per cent abv and are vinified according to classic white wine methods. A slow, thorough fermentation process produces a white wine which undergoes malolactic fermentation (**see p.58**). The wine is then poured into Burgundy-style casks, but these are only half-filled. Rapid oxidation is prevented by a veil (*voile*) of live yeasts (*Saccharomyces oviformis* or *bayanus*) which forms at the surface of the wine, separating it from air. The wine is cask-matured for six years, then bottled in special squat 62cl containers known as *clavelins*. The veil of yeasts protects the wine from direct contact with the air and ensures a slow, controlled oxidation. This produces aromatic elements of ethanol and sotolon responsible for the celebrated '*goût de jaune*' ('yellow taste') that is the mark of these magnificent wines. Alcohol content is the wine's only protection. Fluctuating summer and winter temperatures over six years in the cask favour the development of the yeast veil. Winemakers prefer cellars with fairly low humidity where the wines lose water rather than alcohol. With age, *vin jaune* grows increasingly alcoholic.

Nose

Jura *vin jaune* is an expansive, intensely aromatic wine. At first there are aromas of green walnuts followed by a range of other nutty, more complex scents: dried walnuts, roasted almonds, hazelnuts and walnuts shells. Next to develop are empyreuma notes: smoke, toast, dark-roasted coffee and sometimes cocoa, with touches of liquorice or even strong liquorice sweets. A final touch of spice enhances the overall bouquet: pepper, cinnamon, dried orange peel, cloves.

Palate

The first impression on the palate is one of power and volume. It is impossible to remain indifferent to these rich, full-bodied wines that combine strength, structure and impressive aromatic depth. *Vins jaunes* are the longest wines in the world, with intense, all-pervading aromas that persist on the palate for an incredible number of *caudalies* (see p.51). Thanks to maturation *sous voile* these wines are quite accustomed to co-exist with oxygen. Strongly alcoholic and rich in ethanol, they start life in a *clavelin* (see box left) with the greatest serenity. *Vins jaunes* also have impressive ageing potential: some can be kept for more than a century without the slightest deterioration – indeed their bouquet acquires matchless complexity. At this point, the wine is biologically neutral and will keep indefinitely once uncorked, allowing you to enjoy its qualities at leisure.

Vins de voile...

Jura *vin jaune* comes under four different appellations: the Côtes-du-Jura; Arbois, home of Louis Pasteur; l'Étoile, a small appellation with an excellent reputation; and Château-Chalon, which produces the most celebrated *vin jaune*. Elsewhere, Gaillac still produces very small amounts of similarly produced wines. In Hungary, Tokay is matured in small, half-filled casks from Furmint and Hársevelú botrytised grapes which may, or may not, form a veil of yeasts. The wine produced here is sweet and strongly oxidised. It is in Andalucia in Spain, however, that we find the most famous of all the *vins de voile* – sherry (fino, manzanilla or amontillado styles) produced from the Palomino grape that are grown on chalky soils. It yields a dry, muted wine that is matured beneath a *flor*, the local name for a veil of yeasts.

Sherry, a *vin de voile* from the chalky terrain of Andalucia, can be aged over long periods.

Tasting...
Vins doux naturels and *vins de liqueur*

In the 13th century, Arnaud de Villeneuve, rector of the University of Montpellier, discovered the principles of mutage or chemical sterilisation: the arresting of fermentation by the addition of alcohol. This process was to produce wines rich in sugar: the French *vins doux naturels* and *vins de liqueur*, such as port, from southern Europe.

The alcohol-sugar balance

When tasting a young, sweet wine you will immediately be struck by the combination of alcohol and residual sugar, which can be quite disconcerting. If the range of aromas is rich, then the alcoholic component, which is always present, is well blended and distinguishable only by the richness that it adds to the overall effect. If, on the other hand, the alcohol is dominant, the nose will seem heavy and hot. Likewise on the palate, the substance of a good sweet wine should balance the alcoholic richness. Sugar content is therefore extremely important.

White *vins doux naturels* and *vins de liqueur*

• White or amber Rivesaltes wines

These wines are predominantly based on Macabeu grapes blended with Grenache Blanc and Malvoisie. Wines bottled early are pale in colour with fine, delicate, mainly floral aromas (acacia, broom, fennel, Chinese anise-tree) plus touches of honey or beeswax. Wines matured in tuns acquire deeper shades of gold and copper, plus more developed aromatic

Port was one of the first wines for which production was strictly regulated from 1750 onwards.

notes of hazelnuts, almonds, crystallised citrus and sometimes nuances of roasting.

• Muscats

Muscat-de-Rivesaltes wines are based on Muscat d'Alexandrie and Muscat à Petits Grains grapes. They are pale gold in colour with delightful aromas of exotic fruits, citrus zest, melon, mint or lemon. These are balanced, spirited wines with powerful flavours.

The finest of all is probably Muscat-de-St-Jean-de-Minervois, a floral wine with notes of acacia, lily and honeysuckle, and delicate nuances of citrus that add the finishing touch. The balance on the palate is always exquisitely delicate. Muscat-de-Frontignan, made from Muscat à Petits Grains, is rich and smooth with aromas of citrus, ripe melon and honey. This is a richly balanced wine with a very sweet finish. Greek Samos and Patras Muscats served as models in antiquity and their reputation survived into the Middle Ages. They rarely require chemical sterilisation as the natural

Maturing vins doux naturels (VDNs)

There are two methods of maturing VDNs; each of which will have an effect on the character of the finished wine.

• The traditional method of maturation, especially for red wines, is in half-filled barrels open to the air. The barrels are sometimes stored outside the cellars where the wines will rapidly develop notes of ageing and oxidation and flavours of *rancio*. The colour grows less intense and gradually turns to amber; the aromas take on notes of dried fruits, roasting (coffee, cocoa) and oriental spices; the palate becomes complex and the balance matures. VDNs matured in this way are the perfect accompaniment to blue cheese or chocolate desserts.

• The second method of maturation is similar to the process used to produce vintage port. The wine is matured as for a dry red wine, in a full barrel closed to the air. It is then bottled and aged in a reductive environment. This technique produces more deeply coloured wines that possess aromas of ripe fruits, blackcurrant, spices and tar.

Above: VDNs maturing in the sun in Banyuls. Below: maturing Maury in rows of demijohns ensures a slow oxidation process.

richness of Muscat à Petits Grains grapes is usually sufficient. Patras Muscat is sometimes made from the Mavrodaphne grape. These opulent wines, with their jammy aromas, are made from sun-filled grapes bursting with sugar.

Vins de liqueur or vins doux naturels?

Vin de liqueur and *vin doux naturel* are two distinct categories that have been established by the European Union. The difference between them lies in the process of *mutage* or chemical sterilisation itself:

• *Vins de liqueur*: produced by the chemical sterilisation of fermenting must with *eau-de-vie* (local or imported brandy). Port, sherry and Madeira are all *vins de liqueur*.

• *Vins doux naturels*: produced by chemical sterilisation with neutral alcohol and exclusively made from Muscat, Macabeu, Malvoisie and Grenache grapes.

• *Mistelles*: the French name for *vins de liqueur* that are produced by the addition of wine *eau-de-vie* or *marc* to grape must that is still fresh and unfermented. Three *mistelles* have been granted appellation status: Pineau-des-Charentes, Floc-de-Gascogne and Macvin-du-Jura.

• Malaga

This is a strong, ancient *vin de liqueur* based on Pedro Ximénez, Vidueño, Airén or Moscatel grapes. It is cask-matured for two years and offers intense aromas of caramel, spices, cooked fruit and exotic wood.

• Madeira

Superior Madeira wines are made from Verdelho, Sercial, Bual or Malvoisie. The more ordinary wines are made from Tinta Negra Mole. The method of production is highly original and involves chemical sterilisation followed by heating and almost cooking the wine for three months in *estufas* (steamers) at a temperature of 40°C (104°F). The wine is then matured for several years. Madeira wines have the longest ageing potential of any wines – up to 200 years in some cases. To use Madeira solely for cooking is to miss the pleasure of a marvellously complex wine.

Red *vins doux naturels* and *vins de liqueur*

• Rivesaltes

These traditionally matured VDNs are brick-red in colour with aromas of coffee, cocoa, figs or prunes, quince and crystallised fruits. They present a perfect balance of tannins, sugar and alcoholic strength.

Opposite: vintage port is produced in exceptional years only and must be matured for at least two years.

Vineyards in Madeira are planted on steep, narrow terraces known locally as *poios*.

• **Maury**

Maury VDNs are rich, tannic wines based almost exclusively on Grenache grapes grown on schistous soils. The wines are highly coloured with fragrant aromas of coffee, chocolate, leather, spices and liquorice, plus a well-balanced palate, due to their richness and solidity. Most Maury VDNs are blended traditionally, but you can find vintage Maury wines that offer delicious aromas of red berries.

• **Rasteau**

This appellation in the *département* of the Vaucluse produces a VDN made from Grenache which offers nutty aromas and scents of walnuts, crystallised fruit, prunes and roasted notes. Rasteau VDNs are full-bodied and warm, with a well-balanced, harmonious structure and often intense tannic solidity.

• **Banyuls**

This, the most famous of all VDNs, is made from Grenache grown on steep, schistous terrain on the French border with Spain. Ordinary Banyuls wines are matured in contact with the air but vintage Banyuls are bottled immediately. Ordinary Banyuls take on a mahogany or amber hue and develop aromas of nuts, roasting, leather, cocoa and spices. They have a firm structure on the palate and the strength to age indefinitely, giving them a rare complexity. Vintage Banyuls develop aromas of cherries in brandy, blackcurrants and liquorice. Their tannic strength needs time to mature.

• **Port**

Port is produced from grapes grown on the terraced vineyards on the banks of the river Douro in the north of Portugal. There are many different styles of port, depending on the exact blend of local grape varieties used (Touriga Nacional, Baroca, Roriz, Francesca Cão, Bastardo, for example) and on the method of maturation used (cask-ageing or bottle-ageing). **Tawny port**, in theory, is matured for long periods in tuns or *pipes* (550-litre casks), where it will eventually lose its colour to produce amber-coloured wines with aromas of cocoa, liquorice and orange peel, well-blended tannins and alcoholic strength. (In practice, some tawnies today are aged for no longer than their ruby counterparts, but are made of lighter wines from less intensely fruity grapes.) The wines are then blended to the 'house style', older wines being mixed with crispier, fruitier younger wines. Tawny port can be served as an aperitif, but it is especially delicious with cheese and chocolate desserts. **Colheita** is a rare tawny port created from a single vintage considered of sufficient quality to require no blending. **Late Bottled Vintage (LBV)** is wine from a single year, bottled four to six years after the harvest. Aromas develop in the barrel, but bottling interrupts the ageing process, thus producing a port that is halfway between a tawny and a vintage. LBV is ready for drinking earlier than a vintage port and is a good introduction to tasting vintage ports. **Vintage** port, like Bordeaux or Burgundy for laying down, is produced in exceptional years only, cask-matured for just two years before being bottled. By doing this, the primary fruit aromas and youthful tannins are preserved. Subsequent development in the bottle is a slow process, with the wine retaining its strength and depth of colour. It can age in the bottle for many years, gradually developing a bouquet of unique complexity. The inside of the bottle itself is often thickly coated with sediment and care must be taken when decanting or serving it. Very old vintage port is a wonderful accompaniment to game or blue cheese.

Tasting...
Sparkling wines

Every sense is involved in tasting sparkling wines, even the sense of sound. To improve your appreciation of a wine that may be reticent and timid, or poetic and eloquent, hold the glass close to your ear and listen to the escaping bubbles.

Eye

Sparkling wines, like still wines, should be judged on intensity and shade of colour, highlights, brightness and translucency. The appearance of the mousse and the bubbles must also be taken into account. Carbon dioxide release depends on two factors:

• **Carbon dioxide pressure.**
Mainly determined by the process used to make the sparkling wine, the serving temperature also has an effect. The colder the wine, the more easily carbon dioxide is dissolved and the less pressure it releases. Sparkling wines should never be served ice-cold.

• **The constitution of the wine.**
High levels of surfactants (such as proteins) encourage an abundant mousse. Surfactants work by reducing the surface tension of a liquid, thus stabilising a mousse or an emulsion (as the proteins contained in mustard, for instance, help to stabilise a vinaigrette). The

mousse may be *slight, adequate, excessive, fleeting* or *persistent*. Watch how it behaves in the glass. After the initial mousse has disappeared, consider the slim cordon of bubbles remaining around the sides of the glass. Look at the size of the cordon, the space it occupies and its persistence. Now study the quantity and size of the bubbles that have been released by the liquid.

Pinot Noir is one of the grape varieties used to make Champagne and adds red berry aromas.

Grape varieties used to make sparkling wines

Sparkling wines are mainly based on Chardonnay blended in the *Champenois* (Champagne) fashion with Pinot Noir and Pinot Meunier. They can also be made with Riesling, Chenin, Muscat and Mauzac. Spanish cava is a blend of Spanish and French grape varieties: Macabeo, Parellada, Xarel-lo and Chardonnay.

Nose

The aromas of sparkling wines are driven out of the glass by the carbon dioxide. Primary, secondary and tertiary aromas can be classified with more precision than those of still wines.

Grape varieties used to make sparkling wines produce characteristic aromas: Chardonnay imparts notes of lime blossom, white-fleshed fruits and citrus; Mauzac adds accents of apples and spices; Chenin has aromas of cut hay; Pinot Noir produces notes of cherries, violets and peonies. Wines made by the *méthode traditionnelle* (**see p.86**) have characteristic scents of autolysis, the breakdown of yeast cells associated with the second fermentation which enhances the range of aromas. The wines develop notes of yeast, white bread, brioche, fruit cake, butter and toast. With age, they take on notes of honey, polish and peaches plus hints of spice, or even wood, in the case of the few remaining cask-matured wines.

Palate

Avoid rolling the wine around the mouth as carbon dioxide dulls the taste buds. The wine's attack may be described as *invasive* or *discreet, fine* or *coarse*.

Now analyse the palate as you would a still wine, judging the balance between the acidity, the *moelleux* sensation and tannic content (tannins are present in white wines based on black grapes and in rosé wines). The acidity should be refreshing but not sharp. The wine may be *soft* or *green, supple, fresh, lively* or *nervous*. The *moelleux* sensation is the hardest to appreciate as it depends on the type of sparkling wine. This, in turn, is determined by the *dosage* (the addition of a sweet solution known as *liqueur d'expédition* before bottling). Depending on the amount of *dosage*, sparkling wines are either *brut zéro* or *brut de brut* (which contain no *liqueur d'expédition*), *brut* (dry), *demi-sec* (medium-dry) or sweet. The sugar in brut wines should balance them, especially the acidity which might otherwise be aggressive. A wine with well-judged *dosage* is said to be balanced and harmonious. Too much *dosage*, makes the wine bland.

TASTING BRIEF

The right glass

The glass affects the quality of carbon dioxide release and the wrong one can make the mousse harder to observe. Place different glasses of the same wine on a table and notice how the quality of carbon dioxide release differs in each case. To avoid variations and allow a proper appreciation of the mousse, always use the same glass (preferably a flute, not a tulip glass with a bell-shaped rim). It should be smooth (not scratched) and scrupulously clean.

Making sparkling wines

Sparkling wines can be produced by either the *méthode traditionnelle*, the *méthode ancestrale* or the *cuve close* (tank) method. The **méthode traditionnelle**, formerly known as the *méthode Champenoise* (Champagne method), requires a second fermentation. The first fermentation produces a dry base wine which is run into bottles; after sugar and yeasts are added, the bottles are hermetically sealed. The conversion of this extra sugar into alcohol releases carbon dioxide, thus creating the unique sparkle. The sediment of dead yeast deposited in the process is removed by *remuage* (riddling) and *dégorgeage* (disgorgement). This method can be compared with the older and more natural but less reliable **méthode ancestrale** that is still employed in Gaillac, Limoux and Die. Here, the wine is bottled before fermentation is complete, with some of the residual sugar still remaining. Fermentation then resumes in the bottle until the desired level of carbon dioxide has been obtained. The **cuve close** method is used to produce wines such as Italian Asti Spumante. It involves a second fermentation in closed tanks prior to bottling under pressure.

Two very different types of terrain, produce sparkling wines with strong personalities: the chalky soils of Champagne (above) planted with Chardonnay, Pinot Noir and Pinot Meunier; and the vineyards of Gaillac (right) planted with ancestral vines such as Mauzac.

Tasting...
Eaux-de-vie

L ike wine, there are three main steps to follow when tasting *eaux-de-vie*. The criteria of appreciation are not quite the same, however, as an often overwhelming alcohol content can alter your perceptions.

Eye

Eau-de-vie is colourless on leaving the still, so any colour in the glass must have been acquired during maturation. There is a distinction, therefore, between white *eau-de-vie* that has not been matured in wood (such as fruit *eau-de-vie*) and white spirits (vodka, gin, tequila); and cask-matured *eau-de-vie* (whisky, Cognac, Armagnac and Calvados). These matured spirits become coloured by tannins in the wood. Their colours range from pale straw-yellow to yellow-gold, topaz, tan, mahogany, amber and brown. The degree of colour would be a good indication of the time spent in wood, were it not for the regrettably legal practice of adding spirit caramel, which can give a false impression. While you can be precise about the colour, you cannot draw any conclusions from it. Note the limpidity and brightness of the colour and check for any signs of surface iridescence or undesirable oily traces. Lastly, judge the viscosity of the *eau-de-vie* by the tears it leaves inside the glass.

Nose

Analysing the aromas in an *eau-de-vie* is a fascinating exercise. Genuine enthusiasts may consider the nose for a long time before tasting the *eau-de-vie* on the palate. Proceed as you would for a wine, smelling the *eau-de-vie* in three successive stages: still, swirled and agitated (so as to disturb the surface of the liquor). This will reveal a aromas ranging from the most volatile to the heaviest. Other aromas emerge as the *eau-de-vie* warms up. A great *eau-de-vie* requires airing: it needs time to develop its full complexity. The series of aromas is the same as for wine, with more or less marked tendencies depending on the *eau-de-vie*. In every case, the quality of the distillation is important. The aim of a good distiller is to eliminate a proportion of secondary compounds known as 'heads' (aldehydes, esters and superior alcohol), which are intoxicating and aggressive, and 'tails' (esters and furforols), which are heavy and strident. An *eau-de-vie* destined for rapid sale should contain none of these compounds, but they should be present in small quantities in *eau-de-vie* for laying down. Long periods of maturation in wood mellow the heads and tails, which blend into the liquor and enhance its ultimate complexity.

• A white *eau-de-vie* smells mainly of the fruit from which it is made. How clean and honest is that fruit aroma, and how closely does it resemble the original? Quality in this case is more a question of purity than complexity.

• White spirits are judged on the basis of the clean spice aroma with which they are flavoured (especially juniper in the case of gin), the absence of secondary compounds and well-blended alcohol.

• *Eaux-de-vie* generally present floral, fruit, spice, wooded and empyreumatic aromas along with oily nuances and hints of *rancio*. Note the presence of particular aromas, the complexity of the overall range and the degree to which it stands independent of alcoholic strength.

The golden, delicately amber tones and visible tears of Cognac reflect a wonderful alliance between the spirit of wine and oak.

Palate

Place a very small quantity of *eau-de-vie* (a few drops) in the mouth and hold it still there for two or three seconds before spitting it out. Any traces of spirit remaining on the palate have not had time to numb the tastebuds. The heat in the mouth will cause the sensations to evaporate, thus releasing all their aromas. Begin by examining the alcoholic impression. How strong and well blended is it? Describe the relative strength of that impression using such terms as *fiery, aggressively*
fiery, violent, dry, coarse, penetrating, heavy, powerful, rounded, moelleux, soft, light, weak or *flat*. Now describe the structure and tannic solidity of the *eau-de-vie* (where relevant). Is it: *flat* or *pointed, square* or *round, light* or *heavy, thin* or *rich, sound* or *fleeting, hollow* or *full, poor* or *rich*? What about its tactile quality? Would you say it was *harsh* and *astringent* or, on the contrary, *supple, velvety, moelleux* and *viscous* so as to coat the mucous membranes? List the aromas revealed on the palate by

the warmth in the mouth, including the characteristic scents of particular *eaux-de-vie* (*terroir, rancio,* etc) and any defects (a cooked taste, flavours of caramel, sweat, metal, sourness, mould, soap, grease, yoghurt, rubber or medicine). Lastly, describe the *eau-de-vie's* length on the palate, distinguishing between the aromatic persistence and length due to alcoholic warmth (see p.51). As for a wine, the finish of an *eau-de-vie* may be *brief, short, clean, sound, lingering, rich* or it may *'open like a peacock's tail'*.

On leaving the still, Cognac has a strength of some 70 per cent abv. It is colourless and already possesses unique aromatic compounds which will be enhanced by ageing.

Distillation

This ancient technique dates back to the Egyptians and was rediscovered by the Arabs. It is the process by which the elements in a liquid are separated by vaporisation and condensation. A solution of water, alcohol and other elements is boiled at temperatures of up to 100°C (212°F) until only the water is left behind. The most volatile substances are vaporised at the lowest boiling points and are the first to condense in the condenser: these are the 'heads' with intense, sometimes sharp aromas. The next portion of the distillate, known as the 'middle cut', is rich in alcohol. Tails are the final, least volatile isolates of distillation, imparting heavy aromas. The art of the distiller lies in controlling the temperature of distillation so as to obtain the right proportion of heads and tails for the *eau-de-vie* in question.

A linked or *Charentais* still has a copper boiler with a head and swan's neck.

There are two principal types of still:

The pot still with swan's neck and condenser: this type of still produces *eau-de-vie* by one or more separate distillations (two for Cognac, pure malt whisky, Calvados and certain types of rum; three for Irish whiskey).

The continuous still: this works on the Patent or Coffey Still principle (as used to produce Armagnac, rum, grain whisky, vodka, etc.). An *eau-de-vie* that is destined for early drinking should be purified and contain only the middle cut. An *eau-de-vie* for laying down may contain more secondary constituents which will mellow during cask maturation.

The last drop

This last stage reveals the soul of an *eau-de-vie*. Place a sheet of paper over a tasting glass with a drop of liquid remaining at the bottom. A few hours later, or even the next morning, remove the paper and smell the glass. You may notice aromas that you failed to spot the previous day. This is because certain aromas were held captive by the alcohol – as the alcohol has now evaporated, the aromas have been released.

Tasting...
Armagnac

The Armagnac region, in the heart of Gascony, is shaped like a vine leaf. With its three terroirs and four grape varieties, it produces a range of characterful *eaux-de-vie*.

Quality factors

Armagnac owes its personality to several factors. First there is the *terroir*: the flat, fawn-coloured ferruginous sands of Bas-Armagnac, the *Grand Bas*; the sands, *boulbènes* and argillaceous-limestone terrain of the central Ténarèze region with its steeper slopes; and the predominantly limestone, contoured soils of Haut-Armagnac. Then there are the grape varieties: Ugni Blanc and Folle Blanche as in Cognac; limited plantings of Colombard; and Bacco, a hybrid loved by some, but not by others. Then there is the temperature of distillation – preferably in a continuous Armagnac still – and the careful management of the heads and tails to consider. Maturation is also important; Armagnac should be matured in quality wood from Gascony, first in new-oak barrels then in older wood, alternating between dry and damp *chais* (cellars), and stirring the brandy in open barrels. Lastly, there is the process of reduction. This may be achieved artificially by adding distilled water or low-grade spirit to reduce alcoholic strength to 40 per cent abv. Or, the alcohol may be left to evaporate naturally over time (the portion of a spirit that does this is known as the 'angels' share'). This type of Armagnac, known as *non réduit*, keeps its character despite the drop in alcohol that is encouraged by maturation in a damp *chai*. It has an alcohol content of 42–48 per cent abv.

Armagnac styles

• **Haut Armagnac** brandies are increasingly rare. These are distinctive, sometimes rustic *eaux-de-vie* requiring careful distillation and maturation. A few producers have tried to restore its image and rescue it from oblivion.

• **Ténarèze** brandies have plenty of personality, and pronounced flavours of violets and spices. These are virile *eaux-de-vie*, headstrong in youth but capable of growing beautifully complex with age. They need at least 15 years to soften. The most thoroughbred brandies are produced from Folle Blanche and Colombard grapes.

• **Armagnac** produces elegant brandies that have expansive aromas characterised by scents of plums, zest of orange and vanilla. These are the finest of all Armagnacs. Bacco grapes, grown on sandy soils, express the true nature of Gascony, and produce an Armagnac that takes a longer time to express itself than the others (at least 20 years). Folle Blanche is the source of fruitier brandies that are quicker to open (15 years). Both these grape varieties yield brandies of exceptional quality, which after 25 years develop the notes of *rancio* and varnish that are the mark of a mature Armagnac.

Bacco vines planted on the fawn-coloured sands of the Bas Armagnac (below) yield peerless Armagnacs full of character, whose personality shines in the glass: aromas of crystallised oranges, cocoa, prunes and *rancio*.

Tasting...
Cognac

The production of Cognac is a long and complex process which involves blending brandies of different ages and different origins (crus). By law, no Cognac can be sold until it is at least two and a half years old.

Quality factors

Cognac is double-distilled in a pot still with a swan neck. The first distillate, known as the *brouillis*, is distilled a second time to produce a refined *eau-de-vie* with a high alcohol level (around 70 per cent abv). The alcohol must then be reduced to the marketable level, usually around 40 per cent abv. Nearly 95 per cent of Cognac produced is exported, illustrating the worldwide popularity for this *eaux-de-vie* which, uniquely reflects its *terroir*. The concentric bands that encircle the 'bulls eye' of limestone soils known as Grande and Petite Champagne, are called the Borderies, Fins Bois and Bons Bois. Each *terroir* imparts its own flavours, no matter how much they may be modified by vine cultivation, distillation and maturation in oak. What really gives Cognac its personality, though, is the process of cask-ageing, which may be more or less protracted. With time, the various constituents in Cognac undergo oxidation and the brandy as a whole is enriched by the tannins and aromas of the wood.

Cognac styles

The art of the cellarmaster lies in blending brandies of different ages and origins together to achieve a taste that reflects a particular type, and brand, of Cognac. One of the greatest strengths of the great Cognac houses lies in having the stocks and the buying power to guarantee consistency of taste, wherever or whenever their Cognac might be bought. This is certainly a considerable commercial advantage when selling in large volume, but unlikely to appeal to the enthusiast who delights in diversity and discovery. A few small Cognac houses and grower-producers do bottle their own, personalised *eaux-de-vie*, from a certain age or *terroir*. Tasting these Cognacs is a fascinating, if didactic, exercise that is sure to satisfy the most dedicated curio-hunter.

A great Cognac can present a whole range of complex aromas: vanilla, crystallised fruits, oriental spices, exotic woods, prunes and dried citrus. When comparing a Cognac with an Armagnac, what strikes you most about the Cognac is the sensation of well-blended alcohol. An Armagnac, especially when it has been naturally reduced, always has that headstrong, fiery quality that is so sought after by enthusiasts. A Cognac, on the other hand, softens with maturation until the alcoholic warmth merges with the body of the *eau-de-vie*. Essentially, this is the difference between a very particular style of locally made *eau-de-vie*, and a more international-style brandy.

There are several styles of Cognac depending on the age of the youngest brandy used in the blend: Very Superior, Very Superior Old Pale, Reserve and the exceptional Napoléon, XO, Extra and Hors d'Age Cognacs.

Tasting...
Malt whiskey

There are many ways to make malt whiskey and the notion of *terroir* is relevant. Pure malts should be consumed neat, or with just a splash of still water to release the aromas – certainly no ice or mixers which might hide the unique character of Scotland's finest spirit.

Making malt whiskey

Malt whiskey is produced from barley which has first to be malted, i.e germinated, then dried over a peat fire (the type and quantity of peat used varies regionally, some island peat having high levels of iodine). The malt is then mixed with water from a local source (which can add character of its own depending on whether it runs through peat or granite soils) to form a mash. This is heated to create a sweet liquid called 'worts' which is run into fermentation vessels, where the yeast is added. The fermented 'wash' is then distilled by the pot still method, similar to that used in the Charentes. The spirit produced is aged in used-oak casks that previously held bourbon or, more rarely these days, in casks that once were used to mature sherry. Today, more and more distilleries bottle their malt whiskies separately rather than blend them, with single malt whiskey now accounting for a large share of the market, both in the UK and abroad.

Lowland malts

Lowland malts are distinctively light, with little peaty character. These highly rectified spirits offer a good introduction to an otherwise rather virile domain.

Highland malts

This vast area can be divided into several regions. In the centre is the historic valley of the river Spey and its tributaries, the Livet, Fiddich and

Malted barley mixed with local water and distilled in a pot still... pure malt whiskey can range from light and elegant to robustly peaty.

Lossie. Malts produced here may vary in nature depending on the climate and production method used, but are all classic malts with a good balance of peat and fruit.

Campbeltown malts

This peninsula continues to make a small number of blue-blooded malts made by elaborate distillation methods. These retain the fine balance that earned them their high reputation in the past.

Island malts

The distilleries on the islands off the Scottish coast produce malts strongly influenced by sea air. Peat and seaweed provide an aggressive character that is instantly apparent. These are virile malts for people who enjoy thrilling sensations. Aged for many years and softened by a period of maturation in sherry casks, they belong to that exclusive group of great, characterful spirits.

Tasting...
Rum

Rum is the most widely sold spirit in the world. While it is often confined to cooking, rum can offer distinctive qualities that reflect the method and region of production – the Antilles or the Caribbean, Spanish or English-speaking.

Types of rum

There are two types of rum, each produced by different methods. In the French West Indies and Haiti, so-called **rhum agricole** (agricultural rum) is distilled from fermented fresh sugar cane juice, known as *vesou*. By contrast, in the English-speaking Caribbean, most rum is created by distilling a by-product of the sugar-making process, molasses, which still contains uncrystallised sugar. This type of rum is widely produced throughout the West Indies, South America and the Indian Ocean. Distillation is continuous in practically every case, with the degree of rectification depending on the style of the rum in question.

Traditional French rum

• Agricultural rums from Martinique

The most thoroughbred rums in this category. They vary in style depending on the method of production, ageing and even the type of soil. White rum is not aged in oak barrels and is quite different to the golden, barely wooded rum and old, dark rum that spends varying lengths of time in wood (usually in recycled bourbon casks).

• Rum from Guadeloupe and Marie-Galante

Though less famous than rum from Martinique, Guadeloupe rum can nevertheless provide the consumer with some pleasant surprises.

• Haiti rum

This is a relic of the rum made by the first settlers in the 18th century using *vesou* that is distilled in a pot still, Charentais fashion.

Traditional Spanish rum

Cuba, Puerto Rico, Santo Domingo and Venezuela produce a wide variety of rums made from molasses. These range from very neutral products to more flavourful rums that are aged in wood. The world leader in this category is Bacardi, originally from Cuba but now based in Puerto Rico, with production units in sugar-cane plants all over the world. Bacardi is a very pure rum, mainly used as a base for cocktails.

Traditional British rum

This is the traditional drink of British navvies, who called it 'Nelson's Blood'. It was made from molasses and produced in Jamaica, Barbados, Guyana, Trinidad and the Bahamas. The original version was a robust mouthful that was produced by the addition of '*dunder*' (the residue left in the still) to the molasses, and distilled in pot stills (in the same way as malt whiskey). The liquor obtained was a genuine single rum as embodied in Old Demerara or Old Jamaican rum. This style of rum is now, alas, somewhat rare, rums these days being lighter and altogether more commercial in quality.

Aged in French oak, old rum from Guadeloupe is dark with full-bodied aromas of spices, caramel, light brown sugar and cooked exotic fruits.

Rhum agricole **is distilled from fresh sugar cane juice.**

Dark or old rums are aged in recycled bourbon barrels.

Practise...

Judging the tannic structure of red wines

Wines to be used

1. Beaujolais-Villages

Serve at 14–15°C (57–59°F) and uncork immediately beforehand. Alternative wines: Touraine or Savoie Gamay wines, or a young Gaillac wine.

2. Recent vintage St-Estèphe

Serve at 17–18°C (63–65°F). Uncork one hour beforehand. Decant half the contents of the bottle into a decanter. Decanting has a beneficial effect (see p.24): it boosts a wine that has just spent several years in a bottle. With young vintages, airing the wine accelerates aromatic development and releases them. With mature wines, airing eliminates any notes of reduction that might be noticeable on first tasting.

Alternative wines:

Premières-Côtes-de-Bordeaux or a red Graves wine.

Eye

	BEAUJOLAIS	ST-ESTEPHE
INTENSITY	Light	Intense, almost dark
COLOUR	Bright, fresh cherry fringed at the surface with crimson and even blue-black reflections.	Mainly ruby with a crimson rim and signs of youth.

The influence of the grape varieties

• **Gamay** is an early-ripening grape variety that is suitable for northern vineyards or vineyards at altitude. Granitic soils, such as those north of Beaujolais, are ideal. Gamay yields aromatic, fairly colourless wines often made by semi-carbonic maceration (see p.43).

• **Cabernet Sauvignon** is a late-ripening variety of grape that is grown all over the world, although the best grapes tend to be grown at the northern limit of cultivation, notably in the Médoc region. Cabernet Sauvignon yields highly coloured wines with aromas of blackberries and blackcurrants, exceptional tannic structure and an astringent quality in youth.

Nose

	BEAUJOLAIS	ST-ESTEPHE
FIRST NOSE	Very intense with bright red fruits such as raspberries, plus notes of cherries, strawberries, morellos and redcurrants. Vinification at low temperature using certain types of yeasts can add notes of bananas.	Discreet and even closed.
SECOND NOSE	Floral elements (irises or violets)	Red or black-skinned fruits (cherries, blackcurrants) linked with aromas of cask-maturation (cedar, vanilla, spices). Less ripe grapes can produce hints of peppers. Decanting accentuates fruit content and increases aromatic intensity.

Palate

	BEAUJOLAIS	ST-ESTEPHE
ATTACK	Supple.	Structured.
MID PALATE	Light structure, flowing, even warm.	Substantial with impressive tannic tannic solidity. Strongly astringent, but notice in particular the fine texture of the tannins. Try to distinguish the grape tannins from the spicier tannins of the cask. Decanting improves harmony: the tannins are smoother and the fruit is more intense.
FINISH	Lively and fresh. Little tannic sensation. The aromas linger for a few seconds, recalling the elements detected on the nose.	Intense aromatic persistence dominated by fruit and spices.

Now it's your turn...

Comparing extremes of tannic structure is a good way to memorise the characteristics of wines at each end of the scale. As a beginner, you should therefore try comparing very different wines, such as the range of world wines suggested here. Always follow the basic steps of tasting.

• **Italian Bardolino and Barolo** Bardolino from the southeast banks of Lake Garda is a supple wine produced from Corvina, Rondinella and Molinara grapes. Barolo, from Piedmont, is made from that celebrated grape variety, Nebbiolo. It yields wines of medium colour, fragrant aromas, rich tannins and lively personality.

• **Spanish Jumilla and Priorato** Jumilla, from the arid region of the Levant, is produced from Mourvèdre grapes. Priorato, from Catalonia, is solidly structured wine based on Grenache and Carignan grape varieties.

• **Swiss Pinot Noir** from the Vaud and **Merlot** from Ticino.

• **Californian Blush Zinfandel and Cabernet Sauvignon** Pale-coloured blush wine is based on red Zinfandel grapes that are vinified in the same way as for a rosé wine.

• **Australian Gamay and Shiraz**

Practise...

Judging the acidity and correct tasting temperature of dry white wines

Wines to be used

1. Jurançon Sec

2. Côtes-de-Provence

Both wines should be of a recent vintage so that their freshness and primary fruit aromas are still alive. Ask your supplier for a tank-matured rather than a cask-matured wine. You will need several bottles of each to conduct this exercise in two stages.

The influence of the grape varieties

White wines from the south of France can be classified in two major categories by climate: wines from west-facing vineyards (Bordeaux Blanc Sec, Graves, Duras, Gaillac, Irouléguy and Jurançon Sec) and wines from the Languedoc, Provence or the southern Rhône Valley. The climate on the Atlantic side is characterised by mild temperatures with few fluctuations and heavy rainfall. These conditions favour white wines with plenty of expression and aromatic complexity, but also high acidity. On the Mediterranean side, the warm, dry climate is not conducive to finesse but yields rich, fat wines usually low in acidity (although certain vineyards on north-facing slopes,

	JURANÇON SEC	CÔTES-DE-PROVENCE
Eye		
INTENSITY	Intense.	Medium.
COLOUR	Straw-coloured or golden with green reflections around the meniscus	Distinctly straw-coloured with golden highlights.
Nose		
FIRST NOSE	Exotic fruits (the signature aroma of Gros Manseng grapes): pineapple, lychees, mango and grapefruit.	Floral aromas enhanced by scents of fennel (characteristic of southern French white wines).
SECOND NOSE	Very intense. White-fleshed fruits (peaches, pears). Giving the glass a good swirl reveals hints of spice.	Less intense, more lingering than the Jurançon. Ripe fruits, honey, touches of spice and sometimes a warm, generous note. Giving the glass a good swirl reveals touches of apricot and fresh almonds that add considerable subtlety.

Palette for instance, avoid the effects of extreme heat). These two categories of wine are radically different and therefore useful for demonstration purposes.
The Jurançon Sec appellation is located on steep slopes in the

foothills of the Pyrenees south of Pau, where vines are pruned tall to protect them from frosts. The grape varieties used for dry wines are Gros Manseng, an aromatic grape with high acidity, and Courbu, a more neutral, less lively variety.

Palate

	JURANÇON SEC	CÔTES-DE-PROVENCE
ATTACK	Lively, very nervous.	Rounded.
MID-PALATE	Very fresh but balanced by aromatic strength (fruit series).	Roundness heightened by alcohol content, richness and volume that softens and 'takes the edge' off the bouquet. Aromas of fennel and almonds are expressed to perfection as the wine warms in the mouth.
FINISH	Lingering fruit.	Extended aromas of fennel and almonds.

• More famous for its rosés, the huge Côtes-de-Provence appellation also produces dry white wines. The grape varieties cultivated are found throughout the Mediterranean basin: Ugni Blanc, a neutral and quite lively variety; Clairette, low in acidity but a potential source of delicate aromas; Bourboulenc, warm and full-bodied; and especially the expressive, delicate Rolle.

Stage 1
Taste the wines at 12–13°C (54–55°F), having uncorked them immediately beforehand.

Stage 2
• Serve the Jurançon at room temperature (18–20°C/65–68°F) but keep the Côtes-de-Provence at 14°C (57°F). The Jurançon appears to be less delicate on the nose with increasingly herbaceous elements. The warmer serving temperature shows up the slightest defect in the wine, intensifying the acidity almost to the point of imbalance.
• Then reverse the process and serve the Côtes-de-Provence at 18°C (65°F) and the Jurançon at 14°C (57°F). Now Côtes-de-Provence appears to be unbalanced: the alcoholic impression predominates, emphasised by the richness and *moelleux* quality of the wine. The aromas, however, now seem more powerful.
• Lastly, serve both wines at 6–8°C (43–46°F). This effectively anaesthetises the wines, preventing any further analysis. The aromas seem blocked, the palate is closed, and it is difficult to detect any qualities or defects whatsoever. It therefore makes sense to keep to the traditional practice of serving white wines cool but not ice-cold (see p.22 and p.73).

Now it's your turn...

This exercise is designed to help you define your impression of acidity on a scale that ranges from very lively at one end, to warm and rich at the other. Try comparing the selection of world wines suggested here (always follow the basic steps of tasting).
• **French wines:** replace the Jurançon with a Savennières, a Sauvignon de Touraine or a Riesling d'Alsace. Replace the Côtes-de-Provence with a Gaillac based on Mauzac, a Clairette-du-Languedoc or a Vin-de-Corse.
• **German wines:** choose a dry Riesling from the Mosel and a Pinot Blanc from the Nahe.
• **Italian wines:** Riesling from the Alto Adige and a white Sicilian wine.
• **Spanish wines:** a Rias Baixas and a Penedès. Rias Baixas is a celebrated white wine from Galicia. It is very fruity and essentially based on a local grape variety called Albariño. White Penedès wines, from Catalonia, are usually blended from Xarel-Lo, Macabeu and Parellada grapes.
• **Swiss wines:** a Valais wine based on Arvine, and a Chasselas wine.
• **Australian wines:** try comparing a Sauvignon Blanc and a Sémillon.
• **Californian wines:** a Sauvignon Blanc and a Chardonnay.

Practise...

Judging grape concentration in sweet wines

Wines to be used

1. Sauternes.

2. Jurançon.

3. Arbois *vin de paille*.

This exercise teaches you to distinguish between a sweet wine based on botrytised grapes, a wine based on grapes that have dried naturally on their stalks (*passerillage sur souche*) or one based on grapes dried on straw-covered frames (*passerillage sur claies*). Ask your supplier to recommend a selection of the most representative wines. This won't be cheap, so why not get together with a group of friends? Chill the bottles to 12–13°C (54–55°F) and uncork immediately before serving.

Botrytis or *passerillage*

• The steeply sloping argillaceous-limestone soils and gravel mounds of Sauternes, combined with the climatic influence of the Garonne and the Ciron to the west, together create a microclimate that encourages the development of *Botrytis cinerea*, the 'noble rot' that grows on the skin of Sémillon, Sauvignon and Muscadelle grapes.

• Sunny conditions in the Jurançon favour the natural drying of the grapes. Warm south-westerly winds in the autumn work like a foehn, helping to shrivel the grapes and concentrate their juice. Petit Manseng grapes, with their small pips and thick skin, are especially well suited to shrivelling.

• Straw wine (*vin de paille*) from the Jura is made from Savagnin, Poulsard and Trousseau grapes, unlike *vin jaune* which is exclusively Savagnin. The climate in this pre-mountainous region neither favours the development of noble rot nor is conducive to *passerillage sur souche*. The finest grape bunches are picked when over-ripe and dried on straw-covered frames in a well-ventilated loft. After forceful pressing, these 'dry' grapes are fermented to produce *vin de paille*.

Now it's your turn...

Try comparing the following world wines. Always follow the basic steps of tasting.

• **French wines:** replace the Jurançon with a Coteaux-du-Layon or a *moelleux* (sweet) Vouvray; the Sauternes with a Monbazillac or a *moelleux* (sweet) Gaillac (choose a concentrated *cuvée*); the Jura *vin de paille* with a *vin de paille* from the Rhône Valley (Hermitage appellation).

• **Italian wines:** compare a Tuscan Vin Santo with a Picolit from Friuli and – this should arouse your curiosity – a Recioto della Valpolicella, which happens to be a red wine.

• **North American wines:** compare the ice-wines from the Finger Lakes and Canada with rare Californian dessert wines.

• **German and Austrian wines:** compare different degrees of sweetness in wines made from the same grape variety (Auslese, Beerenauslese and Trockenbeerenauslese), finishing with an *eiswein*. Wines in the last three categories are made from botrytised grapes, whereas Auslese wines are made from *vendanges tardives* (late-harvested grapes).

• **Hungarian wines:** compare Tokay of different strengths, ranging from 3-6 *puttonyos*. Botrytised, naturally dried grapes (known locally as *aszú*) are picked singly. They are then placed in *cuvons* (tanks) where they release a very sweet first-run juice –source of the legendary *Eszencia* wine. The remainder is reduced to a paste and mixed with a dry base for a second fermentation. The quantity of paste determines the number of *puttonyos* in Tokay wines, and therefore their richness. (1 *puttonyo* equals 1.25kg/2³/₄ lb of *aszú* grapes added to a 136 litre/30 gallon cask of dry wine.)

Eye

	SAUTERNES	JURANÇON	ARBOIS *VIN DE PAILLE*
INTENSITY	Sustained.	Sustained.	Sustained.
COLOUR	Golden straw-coloured.	Distinctly straw-coloured with a golden hue.	Antique gold with amber nuances. The richness is more intense than in the Sauternes or the Jurançon.

Nose

FIRST NOSE	An impression of over-ripe grapes, roasted and crystallised fruits.	Impressive strength of aroma even with the glass held motionless; scents of over-ripe fruits; peaches, mangoes and pineapple allied with a unique scent of clover.	Crystallised fruits, pineapple, peaches, raisins.
SECOND NOSE	Characteristic aromas of botrytised grapes: very ripe apricots, spices and pepper, plus floral notes (orange blossom, acacia) and zest of citrus peel. Complemented by hints of dried fruits, followed by honeyed, crystallised flavours.	Honey, beeswax, gingerbread, hazelnuts, praline, spicy notes.	Nuances of jam, quince jelly, prunes, zest of crystallised citrus, beeswax, sweet spices.

Palate

ATTACK	Full-bodied and suave.	Lively.	Opulent.
MID-PALATE	Impressively liquorous; very full-bodied; highly concentrated.	Perfect balance of liqueur and liveliness; sweet but not at the expense of the floral, exotic fruit and spice flavours.	Wonderfully rich with aromas of jam, fruit jellies and rare spices, sustained by waxy notes. Hints of crystallised flavours, honey and sultanas.
FINISH	Opulent, complex and lingering.	Elegantly vivacious. Can be as long as a Sauternes. A great Jurançon finishes with crystallised, honeyed notes plus a range of roasted fruits and spices.	Very lingering, sometimes 'opening in a peacock's tail'.

Practise...
Judging the climatic influence on rosé wines

Wines to be used

1. Irouléguy

2. Tavel

Both the wines should be from a recent vintage so that they still have all their freshness and primary fruit aromas. Serve at 14°C (58°F) and uncork them immediately before serving. You will need several bottles of each wine in order to conduct this exercise in two stages.

Climatic influence

Rosé wines are often produced in tourist regions which sometimes meant the wines were more commercial than traditional. However, some rosés, such as those from the Basque country or the vineyards near the Côte Gardoise, need not be ashamed of their origins.

• Irouléguy, on the north-facing slopes of Aquitaine, at the western extreme of the Pyrenees, is a picturesque wine region planted on steep mountain terraces. Here, where the redness of the soil blends with the green of the wines, the climate is strongly influenced by the Atlantic: mild winters, hot but never torrid summers and heavy rainfall. Rosé and red wines are produced here from Cabernet Franc, Tannat and Cabernet Sauvignon.

• Tavel, rated as the premier French rosé, comes from an appellation that only produces rosé wine. It is located south of the Rhône Valley, on the right bank of the river, facing Châteauneuf-du-Pape. Planted on pebbly soils of sand and argillaceous alluviums, this southern vineyard is characterised by a Mediterranean climate and goblet-pruned vines. Mild winters, torrid summers and periods of drought all combine to produce wines that are packed with sun-filled fruit. Several grape varieties are grown in Tavel, mainly Grenache and Cinsaut, but also some Syrah and Mourvèdre.

Eye

Stage 1

	IROULÉGUY	TAVEL
INTENSITY	Sustained.	Sustained.
COLOUR	Nuances of cherry. Crimson notes from the blue elements in the Tannat create an impression of youth and freshness.	Orange nuances. Grenache often shows signs of development, even acquiring a pale rosé hue. These days, however, the trend is towards more modern colours and a brighter red.

APPELLATION TAVEL CONTROLEE

CHÂTEAU D'AQUERIA

MIS EN BOUTEILLE AU CHÂTEAU

TAVEL

e 70 cl

Jean OLIVIER, Société Civile Agricole, Producteur, 30 TAVEL France

Nose

	IROULÉGUY	TAVEL
FIRST NOSE	Very fragrant, lively and appealing: delicate floral aromas, notes of hawthorn, violets and jasmine.	Intense and warm. Notes of maturity: red berries, crushed strawberries, black cherries, red-fleshed peaches plus white or violet flowers if the blend includes Syrah.
SECOND NOSE	Spices from the Tannat, aromas of ripe black berries. A final swirling of the glass releases peppery notes.	Gun flint and spices. Agitating the wine reveals warmer, cooked notes of soft brown sugar.

MIS EN BOUTEILLE AU DOMAINE
Appellation Irouléguy Contrôlée

DOMAiNE
BRANA
iROULÉGUY
1996

12.5 % vol.   PRODUCE   OF FRANCE   750 ml e

A et J. BRANA, VITICULTEURS - 64220 ST-JEAN-PIED-DE-PORT-FRANCE
L 1297 88

Palate

	IROULÉGUY	TAVEL
ATTACK	Fresh.	Rounded.
MID-PALATE	Very balanced, marrying intense fruit with notes of tannins that add overall structure. Irouléguy rosé wines depend to a great extent on the ripeness of the harvest. Wines from cold, wet years inherit certain vegetal characteristics from the Cabernet Franc (a green taste, sometimes intense, suggesting green peppers). Hot summers and dry autumns produce grapes that add roundness, suppleness and riper fruit.	Supple and impressively full-bodied. Sometimes so robust as to appear rather too warm but for the intense fruit and spices that quell the natural ardour of this typically Mediterranean wine. This is a voluptuous rosé: roundness itself without a trace of sharpness or roughness.
FINISH	Fresh fruit and liveliness.	Ripe fruit, wonderfully generous

Now it's your turn...
Try comparing the following world wines. Always follow the basic steps of tasting.
• **French wines:** replace the Irouléguy with a Béarn, a Tursan, a Côtes-du-Frontonnais, a Bordeaux rosé or a rosé based on Cabernet de Loire. Replace the Tavel with a Côtes-de-Provence, a Vin-de-Corse, a Coteaux-du-Languedoc or a Côtes-du-Roussillon.
• **Spanish wines:** compare a rosé from Navarra with a rosé from Alicante.
• **Californian wines:** taste a Zinfandel rosé alongside a Grenache rosé.

Stage 2
Repeat the tasting process, serving the Irouléguy at 14°C (58°F) as before, but the Tavel at the lower temperature of 11–12°C (52–54°F). The Tavel seems livelier, as the cold destroys all of its warmth.

Practise...
Judging the mousse in sparkling wines

Wines to be used

1. Non-vintage Blanc de Blancs Champagne

2. Non-vintage blended Champagne

3. Gaillac Mousseux (*méthode Gaillacoise*)

Your supplier's help is invaluable when choosing bottles of Champagne. While a Blanc de Blancs may be recognised from the label, selecting a suitable blended Champagne requires an indepth knowledge of the brand. Gaillac Mousseux is not that easy to find outside the region where it was produced but the Hachette Wine Guide contains lists of a selection of producers who keep this tradition alive. Never serve sparkling wines too cold as this may inhibit their aromas.

Production methods

• **Champagne.** This is made from two red grape varieties and one white. The red varieties are Pinot Meunier and Pinot Noir, especially from the Marne Valley and the Montagne de Reims. The white variety is Chardonnay from the appropriately named Côte des Blancs. The grapes undergo gentle pressing to extract a more or less white juice. Pinot juice (Meunier and Noir) contains a few tannins,

but Chardonnay contains none. Base wines made from Pinot grapes are stronger, more robust and vinous. Chardonnay base wines are lighter, more delicate and marked by the aromas of a single grape variety. Wines blended from white and red grapes require all the skill of the producer to maintain the 'house' balance between these two qualities. Champagne can also be produced exclusively from Chardonnay, in which case it is labelled Blanc de Blancs.

• **Gaillac Mousseux.** Sparkling wines were popular in certain parts of France long before Dom Pérignon classified the *méthode Champenoise*. The people of Die filled their glasses with sparkling Clairette that had been famous since the Middle Ages. In Limoux and Gaillac, there was the sparkling Blanquette Ancestrale. Gaillac Mousseux is based mainly on Mauzac grapes. It is made by the *méthode ancestrale* (or *Gaillacoise*): the carbon dioxide in the bottled wine is the result of a single fermentation. The process was developed long ago by *vignerons,* who noticed that fermentation at the end of the season would slow down or even stop with the first snap of winter. If the wine was bottled immediately, the return of

warmer weather in spring would trigger yeast activity causing fermentation to recommence. Carbon dioxide trapped in the bottle produced effervescence but a small quantity of natural grape sugar always remained unfermented. This hit-and-miss method might as easily produce anything from a wine that hardly sparkled at all, to a wine that was positively explosive. Once brought under proper control, the *méthode ancestrale* was, and remains, the source of some real gems. Fermentation these days is halted by repeatedly filtering the wine to eliminate the yeasts. Totally *brut* wines are rarely produced by this method.

Now it's your turn ...

Try comparing the following world wines. Always follow the basic steps of tasting.

• **Spanish wines:** compare a selection of Catalan cava *cuvées* containing different *dosages* (the addition of a sweet solution known as *liqueur d'expédition* prior to bottling).

• **Italian wines:** it is essential to compare the characteristic Muscat aromas of an Asti Spumante or a Moscato d'Asti (from Piedmont) with a Franciacorta (from the province of Brescia in Lombardy), which is more classical in style and expresses notes of Chardonnay.

• **German wines:** compare different types of Sekt.

• **Californian wines:** repeat this exercise using sparkling wines produced by French houses established in California (no Gaillac wine has yet crossed the Atlantic).

Eye

	CHAMPAGNE BLANC DE BLANCS	BLENDED CHAMPAGNE	GAILLAC MÉTHODE GAILLACOISE
MOUSSE	Abundant.	Abundant.	Large, persistent bubbles.
COLOUR	Pale straw-coloured, with an element of yellow.	Deep golden straw-coloured.	Golden.

Nose

FIRST NOSE	Light, on a floral theme.	Red berries and brioche.	Natural fruit.
SECOND NOSE	Flowers, white-fleshed fruits (peaches), citrus (grapefruit), lime blossom, verbena, sometimes tea leaves, irises, fresh grass. This range of aromas is complemented by the aromas of second fermentation: white bread, brioche, fresh butter, fruit cake and toast.	Red berries, hazelnuts, violets, peonies, liquorice, spices, soft fruits. This range of aromas is complemented by the aromas of second fermentation: white bread, brioche, fresh butter, fruit cake and toast.	Ripe apples (the signature aroma of Mauzac), Williams pears, baking brioche, fruit cake made from crystallised fruits. The range of aromas creates an overriding impression of cakes and pastries, ripe fruits and other natural qualities. You can smell the freshly picked fruit.

Palate

ATTACK	Light.	Powerful.	Suave.
MID-PALATE	Very aromatic with a delicate structure. A Blanc de Blancs is the essence of finesse, airy grace and smoothness. The balance between the slightly lemony acidity and the *moelleux* quality always creates a refreshing sensation, giving the wine nerve.	Vinous with robust notes: a blended Champagne is more sensual than charming. Tannins enhance the balance reinforcing the sensation of fullness and volume.	The natural smoothness of Mauzac, a grape low in acid with fruit-driven flavours, combines with the residual sugar from the grape alone, creating a wine that is an Epicurean's delight. There is nothing grand about Gaillac Mousseux, but it does please.
FINISH	Elegant, finesse itself.	More powerful, and longer.	On a theme of natural fruit; modest length.

Using...
The vocabulary of wine

The vocabulary of wine tasting must reflect things with which we are all familiar, and must suggest words that we can all use: each impression should be expressed by a precise term commonly used by all tasters. That said, individual tasters are free to enrich their vocabulary, and to create their own descriptive style.

Analogy

Tasters convey their impressions by drawing comparisons with examples from their own environment. They proceed by a process of analogy: associating a sensation with something material that can be identified by fellow tasters. For instance, when we say that a wine is rounded, we are using a word that does not form part of the semantics of taste, but that we have borrowed from geometric terminology. References to form, bone structure, architecture or the human body are commonly used to describe the body, or substance, of a wine. Even describing aromas resorts to analogy. When we say that a wine reveals an aroma of roses, the taster compares one of the elements perceived on the nose with his or her memory of the scent of roses.

A vocabulary to suit the wine

When describing wines, the rule is quite simple: be brief and to the point with a modest wine; be detailed and even fully descriptive for a more complex wine, including a definition of its style. The description should match the standard of wine, although some great wines defy all attempts at verbal analysis. In that case, adopt a laconic style and sum up the wine in a few well-chosen words: great, perfect or indescribable!

Can you do without a vocabulary?

A technical tasting can amount to a simple positioning exercise, placing each impression on its particular axis. To note acidity, just grade it from 1–10 on the acidity axis (A). A wine may rank as A6 on the acidity axis, T4 on the tannic axis and M2 on the *moelleux* axis. This method can be applied to all elements in a wine, summing up the description in a series of scores. Like a simple record of chemical analysis, the vocabulary of wine is reduced to a handful of grades that allow no distinction between a good wine and a great cru. Only words in all their diversity can do that.

EYE

■ BRIGHTNESS

A wine can be lacklustre, dull, clean, luminous, radiant, bright, sparkling, glimmering or shimmering.

■ RIM

This is the nuance of colour visible around the rim of the glass, which is more or less distinct from the principal colour. The colour of the rim allows you to judge the wine's stage of development. A deep golden rim in a white wine, or a mahogany rim in a red wine, indicates the start of maturation.

■ DEPTH OF COLOUR

A wine can be colourless or pale, clear, dark, sustained, deep, dense or intense.

■ LIMPIDITY

Limpidity may be described as muddy (in the case of a wine that has just been drawn off), opaque, cloudy, veiled, hazy, milky, opalescent, transparent, limpid or crystalline. A cloudy wine is always disappointing, appearing rustic and coarse with no trace of finesse.

■ COLOUR

A wine's colour is usually described by drawing an analogy with flowers (roses, peonies), fruit (redcurrants,

cherries, blackcurrants) or precious gems (garnets, rubies). Such analogies are inevitably general in nature, as cherries come in many shades – as do garnets.

• White wines range in colour from pale yellow to chestnut (definitely a bad sign) with intermediate colours being: greeny-yellow, lemon-yellow (young wines), straw-yellow, golden yellow, buttercup, topaz, antique gold (old and sweet wines), honey, russet, tawny copper, amber, brown, mahogany (very old, spoiled or oxidised wines).

• Rosé wines go from pale grey to brown, progressing from violet-pink through cherry, raspberry, old rose, strawberry, orange-pink, apricot, orange, salmon, brick and onion skin shades along the way.

• Red wines range from bluish to brown with intermediate colours being: purplish-blue, garnet, crimson, ruby (young wines), vermilion, cherry (mature wines) orange, tawny, tuilé, mahogany (old wines), brick, russet (very old wines). A wine may be ruby with an orange rim.

■ VISCOSITY

Viscosity is visible as the wine is poured into the glass: wine may be fluid, flowing, thick, rich, glyceric or viscous. The tears may be obvious, or light.

LE NEZ

■ AROMAS

Three types of aromas can be distinguished during a tasting: primary or varietal aromas (from the grape variety), secondary fermentation aromas, and tertiary aromas or the 'bouquet' due to maturation (see p.34). Identifying the aromatic nuances is the most exciting part of the tasting process, drawing comparisons with flowers, fruits, spices and other natural aromatic substances that you have kept in your memory since childhood: raspberries, roses or vanilla, for instance. When no precise aroma springs to mind, simply record your impressions by grouping them into aromatic families or series: vegetal, floral, fruit, spice and herb, wooded, balsamic, empyreumatic, animal, confectionery, cakes and pastries, dairy, chemical. (See the table of aromas, p.39.) You may notice abnormal odours which indicate poor vinification, maturation or storage: earthiness, iodine, chlorine, rubber, a foxy odour, ethyl acetate (volatile acidity), rancid butter, a stagnant or stale odour, mould, geranium, sulphur, rotten eggs, plastic, styrene, celluloid, lees, cork, leaven, *tourne* (an anaerobic

microbial disease spread by lactobacteria) acetamide, a mousy smell, yoghurt, beer, cheese, vegetables, floor mops, paper, hessian etc. – for more on wine defects, see p.52.

■ SOUNDNESS

Next, you note the soundness of the nose, whether it is clean and free of defects. The nose may be dubious, spoiled, clean, sound, healthy, genuine or pure.

■ AROMATIC HARMONY

Judging the harmony of aromas is more subjective and requires experience. Descriptions may range from unpleasant to ordinary, simple, fine, full-bodied, elegant, refined, harmonious, thoroughbred or complex.

■ AROMATIC INTENSITY

Depending on the strength of aroma emanating from the glass, aromatic intensity can be described as poor, adequate, average or developed. Other adjectives might be neutral, insipid, discreet, closed, aromatic, open, expressive, strong or intense.

■ OXIDATION

When oxidised characteristics are not part of the wine style they are a defect. In this situation the wine could be described as tired, beaten, flattened, *mâché* (lifeless after shipping or bottling), stale, oxidised, cooked, burnt, rancid or maderised. A 'yellow' taste or taste of *rancio*, on the other hand, are legitimate characteristics of *vins jaunes* (**see p.78**).

■ REDUCTION

Genuine reduction odours are always undesirable and include: a stuffy, airless odour, lees, *bock* (beer glasses) or thiol; a smell of stagnant water, raw garlic or onions; a fetid, putrid, decomposed or sulphurous smell; the smell of chicken sheds.

■ AROMATIC PERSISTENCE

This is the length of time during which the aromas are released from the glass and may be easily identified by the taster. (See also 'Finish' under 'Palate' below).

Chemically speaking, aromas are derived from volatile molecules, and the volatility varies with the constituents of a complex aroma. It increases with temperature and the surface area of evaporation. The volatility also varies depending on the weight and structure of the molecules. The lightest of the molecules are the first to evaporate and are the ones that convey an impression of freshness.

PALATE

■ ACIDITY

There are a range of terms to describe the acidity in wine: from flat, soft and flabby for wines that are lacking acidity, graduating to tender, fresh, nervy, refreshing, lively or vigorous where acidity is higher. Wines that have too much acidity can be described as green, harsh, pointed, thin, meagre, biting, sour, hard, bitter, sharp, aggressive, angular, cutting, tart, piquant, stiff, firm, dry or severe.

■ VOLATILE ACIDITY

This obvious defect can be described using the following adjectives: acetous, acetic, acescent, acrid, sour, vinegarish, spoilt, fiery, feverish, *piqué* (acetic or volatile), piquant, vinegary and up-front.

■ AGE

These terms are used to describe a wine as it passes through each stage of its life: young, *nouveau*, youngish, *primeur*, ready, just right, on top form, at its peak, colourless, *mâché*, stale, hoary, decrepit, finished, worn-out, senile, past its best, thin, dried-out and maderized. (See also under 'Future' and 'Development' in 'Overall Impressions' below.)

■ ALCOHOL

Wines are graded on an ascending scale of alcohol content: cold, watery, flat, stretched, watered down, thin, poor, weak, light, balanced, vinous, warm, powerful, generous, robust, heady, strong and spirited. A wine with unbalanced alcohol may be described as alcoholic, souped-up, fortified or fiery, or it may be said to 'have fire'.

■ BITTERNESS

The vocabulary here is limited. Bitter is the only adjective but the taster can refer to plants like sage, gentian, almonds, endives or chicory. A bitter, as in beer, taste indicates pronounced bitterness.

■ ATTACK

This is the first impression created by the wine. It can be described as: false, fleeting or sound, clean, full-bodied, aromatic or intense. You can also use terms that relate to the structure.

■ BODY

This is the very substance of the wine as experienced on the palate. It is structured around one principal axis, either acidity or tannins and, depending on balance, imparts a certain style. It can be simply described by analogy with geometric shapes or, better still, the human body.

• **Geometric analogies:** try to describe the shape that the wine forms on the palate, for example: flat, flattened, filiform, hollow, angular, pointed or twisted; straight, slender, rectilinear, square, spherical or rounded.

• **Analogies with the human body:** a poor structure would be described in such terms as insubstantial, skeletal, thin, slender, slim, weak, puny, skimpy, meagre or slight. A wine with a more commendable structure could be airy, light, slender, sound, broad, structured, well-covered, sustained, solid, square, stocky, corpulent, robust, well-built or sinewy. Too much structure can make a wine seem massive, huge or crude.

The flesh attached to the structure is the substance of the wine. Poor substance may be called gaunt or empty, or good substance could be described as smooth, suave, full-bodied, full, rounded or fleshy. It can have depth, backbone, body, or substance; it may be dense, consistent, cushiony, rich, voluminous or compact. Substance also has a certain fluidity to it. A wine can therefore range in substance from watery, light, smooth, lively, free-running, supple or melt-in-the-mouth, to gummy, thick, heavy, oily, cloying or viscous.

■ BALANCE

The tasting concludes with a summary of the harmony, balance and overall style of the wine. Poor wine can be described as crude, rustic, muted, humble, simplistic, disjointed or even severe. More honourable wines invite adjectives such as peasant, pastoral, young, fresh, *primeur*, appealing, sound, straight, open, accomplished, fulfilled, complete, bracing, virile, ripe, rich, fleshy, opulent, roasted, deep, structured, concentrated, chic, thoroughbred, elegant and grand. Really commendable wines might deserve terms such as subtle, elegant, full-bodied, balanced, harmonious, complex, rich, heady or vigorous. There are as many words to describe wines as occasions to taste them.

■ FINISH

This refers to the gustatory impressions that linger on the palate after swallowing the wine (or spitting it out). A disappointing finish may be brief, short, fleeting or abrupt. A good one might be developed, exceptional, long or complete. At best, it might have enduring length, an 'opening like a peacock's tail' of flavours that linger on the palate long after the wine has passed. (This expression should only be applied to exceptional wines with a finish exceeding 12 *caudalies*, **see p.51**). Great Sauternes, *vin jaune*, white Montrachet wines, the best Bordeaux crus classés, the great Burgundy crus and red Hermitage wines occasionally display this quality.

■ CARBON DIOXIDE

Every wine contains some carbon dioxide. A still wine contains so little that it cannot be detected on the palate. Sparkling wines range from very slightly sparkling (*perlé* or *perlant* – forming a single small bubble that rises to the surface) to *moustillant* (lightly sparkling), sparkling, *crémant* (a wine with soft, creamy mousse), *mousseux* (sparkling, but usually of low quality) and effervescent. If the carbon dioxide is overwhelming, the wine feels prickly or piquant on the palate.

■ SALTINESS

A salty taste is rarely detected on the palate except with fino or manzanillo sherry. It is described as fresh, alkaline, salty or as a taste of the sea air. The expression 'a taste of lye' refers to saltiness, and suggests a defect.

■ SWEETNESS

Here, adjectives range from supple, pleasant, smooth, tender, velvety, softened, melt-in-the-mouth, lively, creamy, rich, sugary, suave, ripe, honeyed and unctuous to soothing, cloying, pulpy, syrupy, soft, flabby or heavy. The choice of words and their significance, will depend on the type of wine – *sec, brut, demi-sec,* sweet or *moelleux* (as in the intensely sweet *liquoreux wines*) Wines made by special vinification methods may be described as: nectar, over-ripe, a taste of straw, *passerillé* or botrytised, as well as bitter-sweet or sweetened.

■ TANNINS

There is a difference between tannic strength and tannic quality, especially in regard to the quality of the texture.

• **Tannic strength:** might be hollow, shapeless, lacking solidity or amorphous; or robust, well-built, well-blended, solid and full of flavour. A wine too rich in tannins is dry, hard, astringent, coarse, aggressive, rustic or overloaded.

• **Tannic finesse:** the texture may be fine-grained, smooth, tight, coarse-grained, loose-grained, consistent, rough or coarse. It can be likened to fabric as you rub it between your fingers, such as silk, velvet, linen, wool, or hessian.

• **Aromatic quality of the tannins:** adjectives include vegetal, metallic, ripe, flavoursome, wooded, vanilla-flavoured, stalky.

OVERALL IMPRESSION

■ FUTURE

A wine with a future already has the required characteristics to age gracefully. One of these is good tannic structure that promises to soften after a few years of ageing.

■ DEVELOPMENT

This is the general state of the wine, accounting for its age. It may be judged visually from the wine's colour and rim, and on the nose by the complexity of the aromas. Development may be normal for the type of wine in question, or it may be too fast or too slow. A wine can be described as young, under-developed, ripe or developed. It reaches its apogée at the peak of its development, followed by decline and decrepitude.

■ CHARACTER (TYPICITÉ)

This is the collection of distinctive qualities that are shared by wines of the same appellation. They are linked to the *terroir* of the appellation (mineral notes, for instance), the grape variety (Gewürztraminer with an aroma of roses, Syrah with an aroma of violets, say), vinification (semi-carbonic maceration in Beaujolais, for example) and maturation (whether cask- or tank-matured).

When to drink wines

WINES	COLOUR	APOGÉE
ALGERIA		
Coteaux de Mascara	rosé/red	1–5
ARGENTINA		
Chardonnay	white	3–5
Malbec	red/rosé	2–8
Merlot	red	2–8
Syrah	rosé	1
AUSTRALIA		
Chardonnay	white	2–5
Cabernet-sauvignon	red	1–8
Pinot noir		
(Victoria, Yarra Valley)	red	1–5
Clare Valley Semillon	red	1–5
Barossa Valley Shiraz	red	3–10
Coonawarra Shiraz	red	3–10
Grange Shiraz	red	5–15
Hunter Valley Shiraz	red	3-10
AUSTRIA		
Grüner veltiner	white	1–3
Kremstal Müller-thurgau		
Auslese	white	1–3
Burgenland Pinot blanc		
Spätlese	white	1–3
Neusiedlersee		
Welschriesling	white	1–4
Wachau Pinot noir	red	1–5
Wachau Riesling spätlese	white	3–5
Riesling Auslese	sweet white	5–15

WINES	COLOUR	APOGÉE
BULGARIA		
Cabernet Sauvignon	red	2–5
Merlot	red	2–5
CANADA		
Ontario		
Chardonnay	white	1–5
British Columbia		
Pinot Noir	red	1–5
Ontario		
Pinot Noir	red	1–5
Ontario		
Ice wine	sweet white	3–10
Québec		
Ice wine	sweet white	3–10
CHILE		
Cabernet Sauvignon	red	2–8
Chardonnay	white	1–5
Malbec	rosé	1–4
Malbec	red	3–5
Merlot	red	2–6
CYPRUS		
Commandaria solera	sweet white	5–15
FRANCE		
Non Vintage		
Brut Champagne	white	1–2
Vintage Champagne	white	2–3
Alsace	white	1
Alsace grand cru	white	1–4

WINES	COLOUR	APOGÉE
Alsace		
vendanges tardives	sweet white	8–12
Jura	white	4
Jura	red	8
Jura	rosé	6
Jura vin jaune	white	20
Savoie	white	1–2
Savoie	red	2–4
Bourgogne	white	5
Bourgogne	red	7
Grands bourgognes	white	8-10
Grands bourgognes	red	10-15
Mâcon	white	2-3
Mâcon	red	1-2
Beaujolais	red	1
Beaujolais crus	red	1-4
Northern Rhône Valley	white	2-3
Northern Rhône Valley	red	4-5
Condrieu, Hermitage, etc.	white	2-8
Côte-Rôtie, Hermitage, etc.	red	8-20
Southern Rhône Valley	white	2
Southern Rhône Valley	red	4-8
Loire Valley	white	1-5
Loire Valley	red	3-10
Loire Valley	medium-dry	
and sweet white		10-15
Southwest	white	2-3
Southwest	red	3-10
Southwest	blanc liquoreux	6-8
Jurançon sec	white	2-4
Jurançon	sweet and	
	liquoreux white	6-10
Madiran	red	5-12
Cahors	red	3-10
Gaillac	white	1-3
Gaillac	red	2-4
Bordeaux	white	2-3
Bordeaux	red	6-8
Grands bordeaux	white	4-10
Grands bordeaux	red	10-25

WINES	COLOUR	APOGÉE
Bordeaux	blanc liquoreux	10-30
Languedoc	white	1-2
Languedoc	red	2-8
Provence	white	1-2
Provence	red	2-8
Corsica	white	1-2
Corsica	red	2-4

GERMANY
■ BADEN

WINES	COLOUR	APOGÉE
Pinot gris Auslese	white	1–5
Pinot noir	red/rosé	1–5
Scheurebe Auslese	white	1–5
■ FRANCONIA		
Pinot gris Kabinett	white	1–3
Ruländer Kabinett	white	1–3
Silvaner Auslese	sweet white	1–3
Hessische Bergstrasse		
silvaner Kabinett	white	1–2
■ MITTELRHEIN		
Kerner Auslese	white	1–3
Silvaner Kabinett	white	1–3
■ MOSEL-SAAR-RUWER		
Kerner Kabinett	white	1–5
Müller-thurgau Kabinett	white	1–5
Riesling Auslese	sweet white	5–15
Riesling trocken Auslese	white	5–10
Riesling Kabinett	white	1–8
Riesling Spätlese	white	1–8
Riesling Beerenauslese	sweet white	5–20
■ NAHE		
Pinot blanc Spätlese	sweet white	1–3
Riesling Spätlese trocken	white	1–5
Riesling Beerenauslese	sweet white	5–15
Silvaner Kabinett	white	1–3
■ RHEINPFALZ		
Kerner Kabinett	white	1–3
Pinot noir	red/rosé	1–5
Pinot gris Beerenauslese	white	5–10

WINES	COLOUR	APOGÉE
Riesling Spätlese	white	1–8
Riesling trocken Auslese	white	5–10
■ RHEINHESSEN		
Müller-thurgau Kabinett	white	1–3
Pinot gris Kabinett	white	3–8
Pinot gris trocken		
Auslese	white	3–10
Pinot gris Auslese	sweet white	3–10
Pinot noir	red/rosé	1–5
Riesling trocken Auslese	white	5–10
■ RHEINGAU		
Riesling Auslese	sweet white	5–10
Riesling trocken Auslese	white	5–10
Riesling Beerenauslese	sweet white	3–20
Riesling Eiswein	sweet white	2–10
Riesling		
Trokenbeerenauslese	sweet white	3–20
■ SAALE-UNSTRUT		
Gewürztraminer		
Beerenauslese	sweet white	2–10
■ SACHSEN		
Müller-thurgau Kabinett	white	1–3
■ WÜRTTEMBERG		
Pinot blanc Kabinett	white	1–3
Pinot gris Spätlese	white	1–5
Pinot noir	red/rosé	1–5
Portugieser	red/rosé	1–2
Sekt	sparkling white	1–5

GREECE

WINES	COLOUR	APOGÉE
Cretan Archanes	red	5
Côtes de Meliton	white	1-2
Côtes de Meliton	red	2-8
Gourmenissa	red	2-5
Mantinia	white	1-2
Metaxa	white	1-2
Lemnos Muscat	sweet white	1-8
Mavrodaphne Muscat	sweet white	1-8
Samos Muscat	sweet white	1-8

WINES	COLOUR	APOGÉE
Naoussa	red	2-8
Nemea	red	2-8
Patras	rosé	1
Rapsail	red	2-5
Cephalonian Robola	white	1-3
Santorini Visanto	sweet white	1-8

HUNGARY

WINES	COLOUR	APOGÉE
Furmint	white	1-5
Lake Balaton Merlot	red	1-5
Tokay 3,4,6 *puttonyos*	sweet white	5-10

ITALY

WINES	COLOUR	APOGÉE
■ ALTO ADIGE		
Chardonnay	white	1-5
Merlot	red	1-5
Pinot noir	red	1-5
sylvaner	white	1-2
Traminer	white	1-2
■ ABRUZZO		
Montepulciano		
d'Abruzzo	red	1-5
Trebbiano d'Abruzzo	red	1-3
■ CAMPANIA		
Greco di Tufo	white	1-2
Taurasi	red	5-10
■ EMILIA-ROMAGNA		
Albana di Romagna	white	1-2
Albana di Romagna		
passito	sweet white	1–5
Sangiovese		
di Romagna	red	2–5
■ FRIULI		
– VENEZIA		
– GIULIA		
Colli Orientali		
del Friuli sauvignon	white	1–2
Friuli pinot blanc	white	1–2

WINES	COLOUR	APOGÉE
Grave del Friuli	white	1–2
Picolit Colli		
Oriental del Friuli	sweet white	1–5
■ LAZIO		
Est! Est!! Est!!!	white	1–2
Frascati	white	1–2
Orvieto	white	1–3
■ LIGURIA		
Cinqueterre	white	1–2
■ LOMBARDY		
Franciacorta	red/white	1–5
Lambrusco	red	1
Oltrepo Pavese rouge	red	1–3
■ THE MARCHES		
Verdicchio		
di Castelledi di Jesi	red	2–8
■ MOLISE		
Biferno	rosé	1
■ PIEDMONT		
Barbaresco	red	5–15
Barbera d'Alba	red	3–8
Barolo	red	5–15
Dolcetto d'Alba	red	1–2
Moscato d'Asti	sparkling white	1
Nebbiolo d'Alba	red	1–5
Roero Arneis	white	1–2
■ PUGLIA		
Aleatico		
di Puglia licoroso	sweet white	2–8
Castel del Monte	rosé	1
■ SICILY		
Alcamo di Sicilia	red	1–5
Etna sec	red	1–2
Malvasia di Lipari	sweet white	1–10
Marsala dolce	sweet white	2–10
■ TUSCANY		
Brunello di Montalcino	red	5–15
Carmignano rosso	red	1–5
Chianti classico	red	3–10
Rosso di Montalcino	red	2–5
Vino nobile		

WINES	COLOUR	APOGÉE
di Montepulciano	red	2–10
Vin santo de Toscane,		
Ombrie	sweet white	1–8
■ TRENTINO		
Caldaro	red	1–2
Trentino riesling	white	1–5
■ UMBRIA		
Torgiano rosso	red	1–5
■ VENETO		
Amarone		
della Valpolicella	red	2–8
Bardolino	red	1–2
Breganze sec	white	1–2
Recioto		
della Valpolicella, Soave	red	2–10
Soave	white	1–4
Valpolicella	red	1–4
■ VINO DA TAVOLA		
Cabernet Sauvignon	red	2–8
Chardonnay	white	1–5
Merlot	red	1–5
Ombrie, Toscane	red	2–8

LEBANON

Bekaa	red	2–8
Kefraya lacrima d'oro	sweet white	1–8

MOROCCO

Beni M'Tir	red	6
Beni Snassen	red	3
Guerrouane	red	2–4
Guerrouane	rosé	1
Koudiat	rosé	1
Boulaouane	rosé	1

WINES	COLOUR	APOGÉE
NEW ZEALAND		
Cabernet Sauvignon	red	5–10
Chardonnay	white	1–5
Chenin Blanc	white	1–3
Muscat Sec	white	1
Pinot Noir	red	1–5
Sauvignon	white	1–2
Sémillon	white	2–8
PORTUGAL		
Bairrada	white	1
Dão	rosé	1
Dão	red	1–5
Douro	red	2–8
Madeira Boal, Malmsey, Malvasia, Sercial, Verdelho	vin de liqueur	15–100
Minho	white	1
Porto LBV	vin de liqueur	5–30
Porto tawny	sweet white	5–30
Porto Vintage	sweet white	5–50
Vinho Verde	white	1
ROMANIA		
Cotnari	sweet white	5-15
Feteasca alba	white	1-2
Pinot noir	red	1-5
SOUTH AFRICA		
Cabernet-sauvignon	red	1–8
Constantia	sweet white	5–20
Merlot	red	1–5
Sémillon	white	2–5

WINES	COLOUR	APOGÉE
SPAIN		
■ ANDALUCÍA		
Condado de Huelva pálido	muted white, solera matured	5–10
Jerez amontillado	muted white, solera matured	1
Jerez fino	muted white, solera matured	1
Jerez manzanilla	muted white, solera matured	1
Jerez oloroso	muted white, solera matured	5–15
Málaga lágrima	muted white, solera matured	5–15
Málaga moscatel	muted white, solera matured	1
Málaga pedro ximénez	muted white, solera matured	1
Montilla-Moriles fino ou raya	white	5–10
■ ARAGON		
– RIOJA		
– PAIS VASCO		
Calatayud	red	1–5
Campo de Borja joven	red	1–3
Cariñena crianza	red	1–5
Cariñena joven	red	1–3
Navarra	white	1–3
Navarra	rosé	1–2
Navarra	red	2–5
Rioja	white	1–3
Rioja	rosé	1–2
Rioja	red	2–20
Somontano	red	2–8
Txakolí	white	1
■ CATALONIA		
Alella	white	1–2
Ampurdán-Costa Brava	white/rosé	1–2
Cava joven crianza	sparkling white	1

WINES	COLOUR	APOGÉE
Cava reserva	sparkling white	2
Conca de Barberà	white	1–3
Costers del Segre	white	1–2
Costers del Segre merlot	red	2–8
Penedés	white	1–5
Penedés	red	3–10
Priorato	red	3–15
Priorato generoso	red	5
Tarragona	red/rosé	1–5
Terra Alta	rosé	1–2
■ CASTILLA-LEÓN		
Cigales	red	1–5
El Bierzo	white	1–2
Ribera del Duero	red	2–5
Rueda	white	1–2
Toro	red	2–8
Toro joven	red	1–2
■ CASTILLA-LA MANCHA		
La Mancha	red	1–4
Méntrida	red	1–5
Valdepeñas	red	1–4
Vinos de Madrid	white	1–2
■ GALICIA		
Rías Baixas	white	1–3
Ribeiro	white	1–3
Valdeorras	white	1–3
■ BALEARIC AND CANARY ISLANDS		
Binissalem	white	1–2
Lanzarote	white	1–3
La Palma	white	1–3
■ LEVANTE		
Alicante	sweet white	1–5
Bullas	red	1–5
Jumilla	red	1–5
Utiel-Requena reserva	red	5–10
Valencia	rosé/red	1–5
Yecla	white	1–3
Yecla ou Almansa	red	2–8

WINES	COLOUR	APOGÉE
SWITZERLAND		
Geneva Aligoté	white	1
Geneva Chardonnay	white	1–4
Geneva Gamay	red	1–2
Geneva Pinot Blanc	white	1–2
Neuchâtel Auvernier	white	1–2
Neuchâtel Oeil-de-Perdrix	rosé	1–2
Pinot Noir from Neuchâtel, Zurich, Geneva	red	1–4
Ticino Merlot	red	1–5
Valais Amigne de Vétroz	sweet white	2–10
Valais Arvine	white	1–4
Valais Dôle	red	1–4
Valais Fendant de Sion	white	1–2
Valais Humagne	red	1–3
Valais Malvoisie	white	1–2
Valais Muscat Sec	white	1–2
Valais Petite Arvine	sweet white	5–15
Valais Pinot Blanc	white	2
Vaud Dézaley	white	1–2
Vaud Épesses Chasselas	white	1–2
Vaud Féchy	white	2–4
Vaud Pinot Blanc	white	1
Vaud Yvorne	white	1–2
TUNISIA		
Coteaux de Carthage	rosé/red	1–4
Coteaux de Tebourba	rosé	1
Muscat sec de Kelibia	white	1
Thibar	rosé	1
URUGUAY		
Tannat	red	2–10

125

WINES	COLOUR	APOGÉE
USA		
Californian Barbera	white	1–2
Californian Cabernet Sauvignon from Central and Napa Valley	red	2–15
Cabernet Sauvignon from Santacruz and Stags' Leap	red	2–15
Californian Chardonnay from Carneros and Monterey	white	1–5
Chardonnay from Russian Valley, San Luis Obispo and Sonoma	white	1–5
Californian Chenin Blanc	white	1–5
Californian Cream Sherry	sweet white	1
Californian Sparkling Demi-Sec from the Finger Lakes and Mendocino	white sparkling	1
		1–2
Californian French Colombard	white	1–2
Californian Gamay	red	1–2
Late-Harvested Gewürztraminer from the Finger Lakes	sweet white	1–8
Californian Grenache Noir from Monterey	red	1–5
Ice wine from Lake Erie, Maryland	sweet white	1–8
Riesling from Washington State	white	1–3
Californian Merlot	red	1–6
Washington State Merlot	red	1–5

WINES	COLOUR	APOGÉE
Long Island Merlot	red	1–5
Californian Mourvèdre from Monterey	red	2–8
Californian Petite Syrah	red	1–3
Californian Pinot Blanc	white	1–2
Californian Pinot Noir from Carneros and Mendocino	red	1–5
Pinot Noir from Oregon and Washington States	red	1–5
Russian Valley Pinot Noir	red	1–5
Californian Late Harvested Riesling	white	1–8
Californian Sangiovese	red	1–5
Californian, Sonoma and Lake County Sauvignon Blanc	white	1–3
Californian Sweet Muscat	sweet white	1
Californian 'sherry'	sweet white	1
Californian Zinfandel from Sonoma, Lake County, Mendocino, Santacruz Mountains	red	1–8

Acknowledgements

Adapted from 'École de la dégustation', Pierre Casamayor,
Hachette Pratique, 1998.

Cover: Scope/J. Guillard
Charlus: 12, 13 (centre), 31 (top), 32 (x3), 36, 38, 43, 45 (top), 49
(x3), 53, 54–55, 61 (bottom right), 66, 73 (right), 75 (left), 76 (x2),
85 (bottom left), 86 (centre). **D.R.:** 6. **L'esprit & le vin:** 20 (top
left). **Photothèque Hachette:** 6, 16. **C. Sarramon:** 87 (bottom).
SCOPE
• **J.-L. Barde:** 16, 18, 19 (top), 28 (centre x 2), 30 (x 2), 37, 45
(bottom x 2), 50 (x 2), 56, 61 (top), 63 (bottom), 64, 71 (bottom),
72, 73 (top left), 75 (right), 84, 85 (top), 91 (top left), 92, 93. • **P.
Beuzen:** 98–99. • **I. Esrhaghi:** 114. • **P. Gould:** 9, 97 (left). • **J.
Guillard:** 4, 7, 10, 11, 13 (top), 14 (x 3), 15 (x 4), 21, 22, 25, 31
(bottom), 34 (x 2), 35, 47, 48, 57 (x 2), 62, 74, 77, 78 (x 2), 79, 80,
81 (x 2), 83, 86 (bottom left), 87 (top), 90, 95, 100–101, 112–113.
• **M. Guillard:** 19 (bottom), 23, 26, 61 (centre), 63 (top), 67, 82,
118-19. • **F. Hadengue:** 86 (top right). • **N. Hautemanière:** 41
(bottom), 91 (right). • **F. Jalain:** 89. • **F.S. Matthews:** 97 (right). •
E. Quentin: 8. • **J-L. Sayegh:** 13 (bottom), 20 (bottom and top
right), 95. • **D. Taulin-Hommel:** 41 (top).

The bottles, labels and estates mentioned in this book are included
for editorial purposes only. They have not been included for the
purpose of advertising.

The editor would like to thank the following companies for
allowing him to use their photographs: **L'esprit & le vin, Tissus
Pierre Frey, Verres Riedel.**

Editorial Director: Catherine Montalbetti
Design: Graph'm/François Huertas
English Translation by: Florence Brutton
Copy edited by: Sue Morony

First published in Great Britain in 2002
by Cassell Illustrated, a division of Octopus Publishing Group Ltd.
2-4 Heron Quays, London E14 4JP
Reprinted in 2004 by Cassell Illustrated

English Translation © Octopus Publishing Group Ltd 2002
© Hachette Livre (Hachette Practique) 2001

Distributed in the United States of America by
Sterling Publishing Co., Inc.,
387 Park Avenue South, new York, NY 10016-8810

A CIP catalogue record for this book is available from the British
Library.

ISBN 0 304 36408 8
EAN 9780304364084

Printed in China

Cassell Illustrated
A Division of the Octopus Publishing Group Ltd
2–4 Heron Quays, London E14 4JP